HOW BIRDS MIGRATE

HOW BIRDS MIGRATE

Paul Kerlinger

Illustrated by Pat Archer

STACKPOLE
BOOKS

Published by
STACKPOLE BOOKS
5067 Ritter Road
Mechanicsburg, PA 17055

Printed in the United States of America

Cover design by Caroline Miller
Computer graphics by Sandra M. Blair

First edition

10 9 8 7 6 5 4 3 2

Library of Congress Cataloging-in-Publication Data

Kerlinger, Paul.
    How birds migrate / Paul Kerlinger ; illustrated by Pat Archer. —
1st ed.
      p.   cm.
    Includes bibliographical references and index.
    ISBN 0-8117-2444-1
    1. Birds—Migration. I. Title.
QL698.9.K47   1995
598.252'5—dc20   95-7238
                                                        CIP

To Jane

CONTENTS

PREFACE

THAT A SWAINSON'S HAWK, WEIGHING ABOUT 2 POUNDS, MIGRATES from its breeding site on the prairies of Saskatchewan to its wintering grounds in southern Argentina is amazing. That a Semipalmated Sandpiper, weighing only an ounce, migrates from the Canadian tundra to northern South America is even more difficult to comprehend. That a Ruby-throated Hummingbird, weighing only ⅙ ounce, can fly from its nesting area in a New Hampshire forest to its wintering grounds in Costa Rica is almost unbelievable. Yet these birds and thousands of others routinely undertake perilous and difficult journeys. The number of migrants involved cannot even be estimated. It is certainly in the billions!

I am not alone in my amazement. Hundreds of scientists, millions of birdwatchers, and countless other people from around the world want to know more about the epic flights made by birds. Today we are lucky that technology and human interest in migration have provided us with a wealth of information about how and why birds migrate.

This book is for those who are fascinated by the migration of birds. I hope to fill a gap in the literature that exists between technical and popular presentations. Popular accounts of migration often lack substance, which leaves the reader wanting more. At the other extreme, scientific accounts present information that is so detailed or so narrowly focused that the reader loses interest and never fully grasps the topic. Bridging the gap between popular and scientific writing is tricky, but it is the only way to provide enough information for the reader to truly appreciate and understand migration.

To help people better understand how and why birds migrate, each chapter addresses a single aspect or component—the altitude of migration, flocking behavior, flight speed, orientation—isolated from other aspects of migration. Those readers who are familiar with my earlier volume, *Flight Strategies of Migrating Hawks,* will recognize parallels between that volume and this book. There are also some similarities between this work and Tom Alerstam's book, *Bird Migration;* the major differences are that this book is nontechnical and does not focus on one taxonomic group of birds.

Anyone who reads such magazines as *National Geographic, Scientific American, Smithsonian, Natural History, Bird Watcher's Digest,* or *Audubon* should find this book readable. Most readers may have some knowledge about birds and migration, but even the novice birder should find much of interest. While presenting the relevant factual material about the birds, I have also attempted to show how scientists have studied migration and how difficult their field is. The case studies examine individual species or actual research projects conducted by migration researchers.

Migration research has never been dominated by the work of one individual or a single institution. Instead, hundreds of different people working at hundreds of places have contributed to our knowledge of migration. It is unfortunate that all of these researchers and institutions could not be acknowledged. The large number of people and institutions attests to the immensity of the field and the degree of interest on the part of researchers. With such a large number of people studying migration, we can look forward to many discoveries and much new information in the near future.

This book attempts to provide a world view of migration, but it is, I admit, somewhat biased to migration in North America and Europe. Where possible, I have cited migration phenomena from Asia, South America, and elsewhere, but there is less information on migration outside of North America and Europe as well as a scarcity of good research from those areas.

For those readers who wish to learn more about migration, I have included a section of resources at the end, with some fifty books and articles that will give the reader more detailed information.

If, when you have read this book, you come away with a feeling of excitement about migration and an awe for how birds migrate, I will have been successful.

ACKNOWLEDGMENTS

I HAVE LEARNED ABOUT MIGRATION FROM MANY PEOPLE, AS WELL AS from the birds themselves. I owe a great debt to Frank Moore, who helped with the conceptual approach for this book and gave me guidance. Whenever I hit a stumbling block, I called Frank. Sid Gauthreaux, Ken Able, and Ross Lein supported and encouraged my research efforts. I also wish to thank the migration research community, whose hard work and dedication have provided the information in this volume.

A group of people who cannot be overlooked are the birders who have contributed and continue to contribute to our overall understanding of migration. To this group, I owe a special debt. Thanks go to the Brit Boys (Richard Crossley, Paul Holt, and Julian Hough), Pete Dunne, Vince Elia, Tony Leukering, Bob Barber, Clay Sutton, Dave Wiedner, Dave Ward, Joe Palumbo, Fred Mears, Dave Sibley, Katy Duffy, Patrick Matheny, Jim Brett, Bill Glaser, Rich Kane, James Dowdell, Jeff Bouton, Chris Schultz, Bill Clark, and Patricia Sutton.

Trying to learn about migration in an academic institution is rewarding but needs the balance of general fieldwork. My interactions with Pete Dunne at Cape May in the early 1980s provided important field experiences and a sounding board for ideas.

For reading portions of earlier drafts of this book and providing helpful comments, I thank Vince Elia, Rosemarie Widmer, A. Richard Turner, Jack Connor, and Frank Moore.

Funding for the writing phase of this book came from several sources. Members of New Jersey Audubon Society and Cape May Bird Observatory provided me with an income and the time to write. Without the generosity and continuing care of members, nonprofit organizations like NJAS and CMBO could not exist. I thank them and want them to know that those of us who work for these organizations really appreciate their contributions of funds and time. The NJAS Board of Directors was most generous regarding my devoting time to writing, and they understood my needs as a researcher. I am indebted to Tom Gilmore, Executive Director of New Jersey Audubon Society, who permitted me to take time to write.

ONE

The Reason Birds Migrate

WHEREVER THERE ARE BIRDS, THERE IS MIGRATION. ARCTIC BIRDS migrate, as do tropical birds. So do birds that live in mountains, forests, prairies, deserts, islands, and just about any habitat you can imagine. Migration, that part of an animal's life characterized by geographic movements, is an incredibly diverse behavior, an adaptation that has been shaped by natural selection.

Those of us who live in temperate climates usually think of migration as the seasonal movement of birds during spring and fall to avoid harsh weather. This is only partly correct. Migration evolved as a way for birds to exploit resources that are seasonally abundant and avoid times when or places where resources are scarce or weather is very harsh. Many species can tolerate cold temperatures if food is plentiful; when food is not available they must migrate.

In temperate and arctic regions of the Northern Hemisphere, food is abundant during a short growing season. During June and July, the Arctic is teeming with both terrestrial and aquatic insect life. It is during this time that many species of birds breed. Pectoral Sandpipers and other shorebirds that arrive on the tundra in early June rely on a flush of insects to accumulate energy and calcium for eggs as well as to feed their young. These same birds also migrate to other places when food is abundant—to the Bay of Fundy in autumn and the Delaware Bay during spring, for example.

Many other birds, including raptors, egrets, waterfowl, loons, grebes, cranes, owls, and storks, migrate to northern latitudes to breed. Hundreds of species of songbirds travel to the northern forests of North America, Europe, and Asia to feast on the seasonal flush of insects. Scarlet Tanagers are an excellent example. Like the shorebirds, they spend only a portion of the year in the temperate zone. By October, many of these birds have left the northern forests for more southerly climes.

TYPES OF MIGRATION PATTERNS

Most birds that inhabit temperate and arctic latitudes migrate according to one of three patterns: complete, partial, or irruptive.

Complete Migration

Many North American shorebirds, tanagers, warblers, vireos, orioles, hummingbirds, flycatchers, and thrushes are complete migrants. That is, virtually all members of the species leave their breeding range during the nonbreeding season. Most complete migrants breed in northern temperate and arctic areas of North America, Europe, and northern Asia. Only a few are known from South America, Africa, or Australia. Among the 285 or so species of hawks in the world, for example, complete migrations are limited to those that breed in the Northern Hemisphere, mostly north of 30 degrees north latitude; no diurnal raptors breeding in Africa and South America are complete migrants. Why the difference? In the Northern Hemisphere, there are significant land masses north of 55 degrees latitude that can host hundreds of species of breeding birds, but there are almost no land masses in the Southern Hemisphere south of 55 degrees.

Complete migrants may travel incredible distances, sometimes more than 15,000 miles (25,000 kilometers) per year. The wintering areas for most complete North American migrants are South and Central America, the Caribbean basin, and the southernmost United States. In Europe and Asia these species fly into Africa, southern

The migration of Rough-legged Hawks is said to be complete because all individuals leave the breeding range.

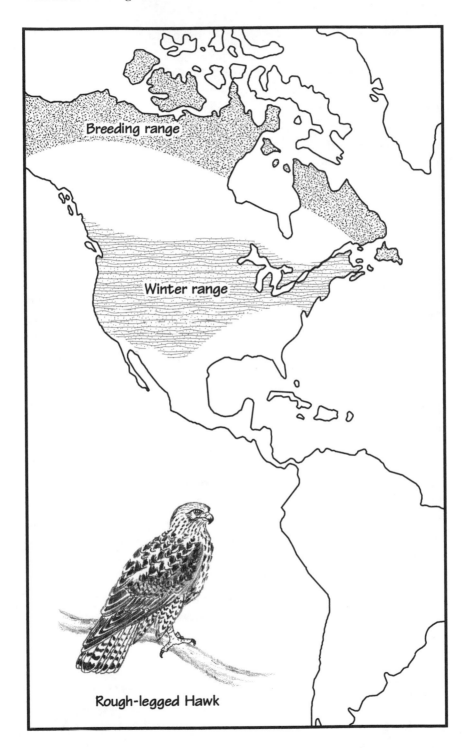

Breeding range

Winter range

Rough-legged Hawk

Asia, and the Pacific basin. Many complete migrants cross the equator.

The Eastern Wood Pewee and Swainson's Hawk are complete migrants. Pewees breed in forests from southern Manitoba east to the southern Canadian Maritimes and south to the Gulf coast of the United States. In winter they all leave North America to winter in Central and South America. The Swainson's Hawk is one of fewer than twenty species of hawks that undertake complete migrations. From their breeding range in western North America (from Alberta south into Arizona and Texas), they fly into Central and South America each autumn. A marvelous banding study by Stuart Houston, a physician from Saskatchewan who studies birds as an avocation, shows the migration pathway and wintering areas of Saskatchewan breeders. Houston has banded thousands of hawks during his many years of banding. Between the center of their breeding range in North America and the probable center of their wintering range, Swainson's Hawks travel about 5,000 miles (8,000 kilometers) round-trip each year. Every winter only a few aberrant Swainson's Hawks are found in the United States.

Partial Migration

By far the most common type of migration, partial migration is characterized by seasonal movements away from a breeding range by some, but not all, members of a species. There is, then, an overlap between nonbreeding and breeding ranges of the species. Like complete migrants, partial migrants take advantage of seasonally abundant food. Species like the Red-tailed Hawk and Herring Gull are partial migrants over much of their North American ranges. In eastern Canada, most members of these species migrate south for the winter, and only a few birds winter in the north.

Bewick's Wren is a good example of a North American partial migrant. These wrens are year-round residents from southern Illinois to the Gulf coast. East of the Mississippi their breeding range extends

Most Song Sparrows migrate south for the winter, but some individuals remain in their breeding areas; the migration of this species is partial.

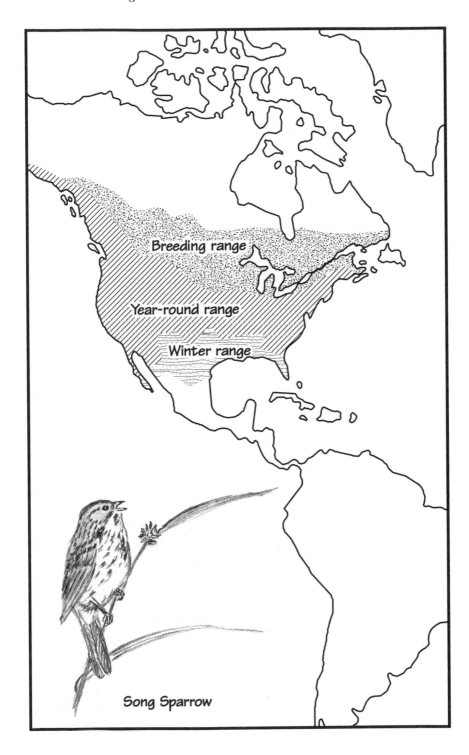

Breeding range

Year-round range

Winter range

Song Sparrow

northward, into southern Wisconsin and Minnesota, but they are absent from this part of their range in winter. A South American analogue to this migration pattern is the White-rumped Swallow, which breeds in Uruguay, Paraguay, Bolivia, southern Brazil, and northern Argentina. During the austral winter (June to August), White-rumped Swallows are nearly absent from the pampas of Argentina and Uruguay, the southernmost portion of their breeding range. They move northward as far as Peru but are present year-round in Brazil, Bolivia, and much of the northern part of their range.

Irruptive Migration

Migrations that are not seasonally or geographically predictable are termed irruptive. Such migrations may occur one year but not again for many years. The distances and numbers of individuals involved are also less predictable than with complete or partial migrants. In some years irruptions (as irruptive migrations are called) can be over long distances and involve many individuals, or they can be short and involve only a few. The Great Gray Owl is an irruptive migrant, migrating southward only occasionally and in numbers that vary greatly. Before the winter of 1979–80, the birds rarely appeared in the northeastern United States, but during that winter more than a hundred were seen. How many lived to return to the northern forest is not known.

Northern finches and crossbills are irruptive migrants. As with partial and complete migration, these movements are adaptive. Without them the future reproductive success (called fitness by evolutionary biologists) of the individuals involved would be reduced.

Some scientists maintain that irruptive species are food specialists. For example, some northern finches in North America eat the seeds of only a few trees. When these seeds are not available, entire populations of finches leave the boreal forest to find food farther south. Similarly, such predators as the Northern Shrike depend on lemmings during the breeding season. When lemming populations crash, the shrikes make irruptive migrations into temperate areas.

In some years Red Crossbills migrate south, in others they do not migrate at all. Migration that varies from year to year is said to be irruptive.

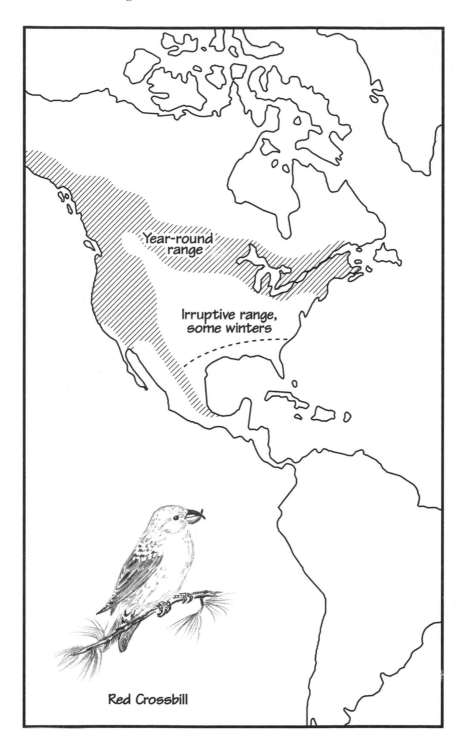

Year-round range

Irruptive range, some winters

Red Crossbill

> ## CASE STUDY
>
> *Irruptive Migrants:*
> *Pine Siskin and Red-breasted Nuthatch.*

RIGOROUS ANALYSIS AND USE OF NATIONAL AUDUBON SOCIETY'S Christmas Bird Count data have shown massive irruptions of several species that migrate from their breeding areas in the forests of Canada and the northern United States. Pine Siskins and Red-breasted Nuthatches are two such northern seedeaters that have irruptions. In the case of Pine Siskins, the irruptions are thought to occur every other year, depending on the absence or abundance of the seeds they eat. The analyses of some species have shown that some winter irruptions are continentwide. ■

Variations

To categorize a species as a complete or partial migrant is not always easy, since there is usually some variation in migratory behavior among individual birds. The Peregrine Falcon, for example, is a nearly cosmopolitan species, breeding on all continents except Antarctica. Some of its populations are complete migrants, others are partial migrants, and still others do not migrate. In North America, the tundra subspecies *(Falco peregrinus tundrius)* that breeds in arctic Canada, Alaska, and Greenland is completely migratory. All individuals leave the breeding range, and most migrate south of the United States. Peregrines that breed in the continental United States *(Falco peregrinus anatum)* are only partially migratory, with some individuals not migrating away from the breeding area at all. Finally, some tropical and subtropical Peregrines do not migrate. This type of variation within a species is not unusual.

> ## CASE STUDY
>
> *Rainy Season–Dry Season Migrants:*
> *Wahlsberg's Eagle and Grasshopper Buzzard.*

THE RAINY SEASON IN AFRICA AND SOME OTHER CONTINENTS PROMPTS mass movements of many birds, including raptors. The migration of many African hawks, eagles, and falcons is timed to exploit food made seasonally abundant by rainfall. The Wahlsberg's Eagle migrates to the southern part of Africa to breed during the dry season and flies back north for the wet season, after breeding. The Grasshopper Buzzard does just about the opposite, breeding in the northern part of its range and migrating south to spend the dry season—October through March. These different migration strategies deserve extensive study. ■

| **CASE STUDY** | *A Longitudinal, East-West Migrant: White-winged Scoter.* |

MOST NORTH-SOUTH MIGRATIONS HAVE AN EAST-WEST COMPONENT, but some species may migrate farther east or west than north or south. The White-winged Scoter breeds in the area from Alaska east and southward to western Ontario, yet it is a regular migrant down the East Coast of the United States: it arrives there by flying almost due east. Other species that live in central North America also have a similar easterly component to their migration. ■

| **CASE STUDY** | *Leapfrog Migrants: Peregrine Falcon and Common Buzzard.* |

IN MANY SPECIES OF MIGRANTS, INDIVIDUALS FROM THE MOST NORTHerly populations fly farther south than those from more southerly populations. Called leapfrog migration, this pattern is most common among species whose populations are spread over a wide range of latitude. Among Peregrine Falcons, for example, tundra-breeding birds fly to the Neotropics, and temperate breeders do not migrate or migrate only short to medium distances. A leapfrog pattern is also evident in the Common Buzzard, which inhabits Europe and Asia. Birds from the most northerly regions, like Sweden and Germany, fly to Africa for the winter, and those that breed in southern Europe (Spain) may overwinter in Europe. ■

Such examples illustrate the diversity of migration. Migration can be as short as 20 miles (32 kilometers) or longer than 20,000 miles (32,000 kilometers) round-trip. The timing and direction of flight can vary greatly, even within a single species. The traditional north-south flights most familiar to us inhabitants of temperate climes in the Northern Hemisphere are only one type of migration.

Differences in migratory behavior and pattern within a species are evident among geographic populations, age classes, sex classes, or combinations of these. Called differential migration, this variation is manifested by differences in seasonal timing of migration and range during the nonbreeding season. Differences in distance of migration or wintering area between age or sex classes usually involve a species that is a partial migrant. Among complete migrants there seems to be a greater mixing of age and sex classes during the nonbreeding period, and differential migration has not been documented as often.

| CASE STUDY | *Female Dark-eyed Juncos Migrate Farther South than Males.* |

RESEARCHERS AT INDIANA UNIVERSITY HAVE STUDIED THE MIGRATORY behavior and ecology of Dark-eyed Juncos since the 1970s. Because of this work, we may know more about this species' migration than that of any other North American species. Fieldwork at many sites in eastern North America demonstrates that female juncos migrate farther south than males. After breeding in the northern forests this common finch flies south and can be found over a large portion of the eastern United States during winter. Females tend to migrate farther than males and make up a greater proportion of the population in places like southern Indiana than in southern Ontario, where males predominate. ■

| CASE STUDY | *Immature Male Snowy Owls Migrate Farther South than Adult Females.* |

ROSS LEIN OF THE UNIVERSITY OF CALGARY AND I STUDIED THE DIF-ferential pattern of migration among the four age-sex classes (adult males, adult females, immature males, immature females) of North

American Snowy Owls. Based on the collection locations of more than eight hundred museum skins, we concluded that immature males migrate farthest south and adult females remain farthest north in winter. There was overlap among the four age-sex classes in distribution, so findings were based on differences in percentage. South of 45 degrees north latitude immature males accounted for 46 percent of museum skins, and immature females accounted for another 40 percent. Only 10 to 15 percent of the birds found on the Great Plains of Canada during the winter were immature males. During fifteen years of fieldwork in Alberta, Lein has noted a large proportion of adult females on his study sites. Additional evidence for a differential migration of Snowy Owls comes from more than seventy Snowy Owls banded in the winter of 1991–92 in upstate New York along the south shore of Lake Ontario. About 85 percent of the owls were immatures, with immature males predominating. Differential migration by age and sex among these partial migrants is obvious. ■

CASE STUDY	*Immature Herring Gulls Migrate Farther South than Adults.*

THE BEST DOCUMENTATION OF DIFFERENTIAL MIGRATION IS A STUDY OF Herring Gull migration by Frank Moore, then a graduate student at Clemson University. He analyzed winter recovery locations of Herring Gulls banded at breeding colonies on the Great Lakes. He showed that the migration of Herring Gulls became progressively shorter as they grew older. First-year birds migrated to the Atlantic coast as far south as Florida. Fourth-year birds rarely migrated as far south as the Carolinas. These findings imply that site fidelity is low, meaning that individuals do not winter in the same place year after year. After the first year or two, however, some of these birds could return to the same wintering sites year after year. The pattern demonstrated by Herring Gulls is one of the clearest yet found of adults wintering far to the north of immatures. ■

Breeding at higher elevations of the Appalachian Mountains of the eastern United States, the Carolina Junco is a short-distance, ele-

vational migrant. Its migration is often less than 20 miles (32 kilometers) down the mountains to lower elevations, but even this short
movement permits the species to escape cold weather and snow on
the mountaintop during winter. In late winter some males return to
their lofty breeding sites, but they may not stay. If conditions are
acceptable, they remain to secure good nest sites. If the weather is bad,
they fly back down the mountain until it improves. The short distance
between breeding and wintering sites permits these birds to test the
conditions at the mountaintop without wasting enormous amounts of
energy, as would be required by longer-distance migrants.

Among partial migrants, immature birds usually migrate farther
than adults. The pattern of differences between males and females is
not as pronounced. In some species females migrate farther to wintering sites; in others males do. When both age and sex are considered,
the pattern is often not clear because both play a role in determining
which individuals migrate farther.

Why differential migration exists and how it evolved are two of
the hottest questions in migration biology. One explanation, called
the *social dominance hypothesis,* states that some individuals will dominate a resource, usually food, making subordinate individuals migrate
farther. This usually means bigger birds and adults will dominate
smaller birds and immatures, which must fly farther to find food.
This could explain why adults winter closer to the breeding area
than young birds. Migration is costly, and it does not pay to fly farther than necessary. This also explains why the larger sex of some
species winters north of the smaller sex.

Other biologists believe that by wintering on or close to the
breeding site, an individual does not need to fly as far in spring and
can therefore acquire the best breeding site upon arrival. This
hypothesis would explain why in some species males winter north of
females.

Neither of those explanations works for all species, but for a
given species one or the other may explain differential migration.
For example, among species that do not breed in their second year,
social dominance may operate on first-year birds but not on adults.
Suffice it to say that evolution has shaped these patterns differently
among species.

RARE BIRDS AND BIRDS OUT OF RANGE

Birders delight in finding rare birds and in spotting a common bird outside its normal breeding, migration, or nonbreeding range. Birders in such places as the Scilly Isles off the southwest coast of Great Britain venture forth in autumn in hopes of adding "ticks" (new birds) or "lifers" to their life lists—usually a North American or Asian migrant that is out of its normal migratory range. A Gray-cheeked Thrush or a Magnolia Warbler is indeed a special bird at such locations, because they are normally found in North America. In the same way, the sighting of a Eurasian Purple Gallinule in someone's backyard in Wilmington, Delaware, or a Western Kingbird or Western Tanager in Cape May, New Jersey, is puzzling. How do birds find themselves so far from their normal range?

The Eurasian Purple Gallinule that arrived in Wilmington in the autumn of 1990 thrilled many birders. It could not have made the flight under its own power. Instead, it cither crossed the ocean on a ship or was released from captivity somewhere near Wilmington. One field guide states that this bird rarely migrates, and when it does, it may travel on foot! We will probably never know how it came to be in Delaware.

A Canadian biologist, Ian McLaren, examined the occurrence of dozens of "out-of-range" or "vagrant" birds found over several decades in Nova Scotia. He hypothesized that many South American birds, such as Fork-tailed Flycatchers, arrived in Nova Scotia after storms or after prolonged southerly or southeasterly winds. His meticulous analyses included evaluating continental weather maps for the days before a rare species arrived. The weather usually explained the presence of rare birds.

As a graduate student, David DeSante, now of the Bird Population Institute, also examined out-of-range birds. He studied mostly eastern songbirds, particularly wood warblers, because he wanted to explain their arrival on the Pacific coast during autumn migration. He suggested a novel hypothesis—mirror-image orientation, whereby the "compasses" of eastern migrants became reversed as if they were viewed in a mirror. The result of this reversal brought them to the West Coast instead of the Midwest or the East Coast of North America.

One of the simplest explanations for some out-of-range birds, however, relies on simple statistics. Any large population is likely to have a few aberrant individuals that deviate greatly from the norm in weight, speed, plumage, or migratory orientation. If a common species normally migrates to the southeast, there are bound to be a few individuals who will fly to the southwest or to the east; these are the birds that may find their way to strange places. Couple this with the large number of birders who go to places like Cape May or coastal California, where birds congregate in large numbers, and the probability of finding aberrant individuals increases. These are the reasons rarities occur at a higher rate at these places than elsewhere.

There are, no doubt, many explanations for finding birds out of their normal migratory ranges. Some may have aberrant "compasses" and some may be blown by wind and weather. Vagrants and rarities will always fascinate birders.

CASE STUDY	*An Austral Migrant: Fork-tailed Flycatcher.*

FORK-TAILED FLYCATCHERS ARE ONE OF MANY SOUTH AMERICAN BIRD species that, like the White-rumped Swallow, migrate northward during the austral winter, a mirror image of normal migration in North America. Some move to Trinidad, off the northern coast of South America, and others fly into Central America. Occasionally, Fork-tailed Flycatchers overshoot their normal wintering areas and are seen as far north as New Jersey or Nova Scotia. Other South American migrants, such as the Large-billed Tern, arrive in North America after overshooting their destinations in northern South America. They may have been blown northward by a storm or strayed from their migratory route because of an aberrant migratory compass. ∎

THE EVOLUTION OF BIRD MIGRATION
Dozens of scientists and birders have attempted to explain or trace the evolution of bird migration, but none of their theories have been entirely plausible or widely accepted. Explanations involve glacia-

tion, continental drift, changing climatic patterns, extending dispersal distance, northern ancestral homes, southern ancestral homes, and
combinations of these.

Although biologists will not agree on which hypothesis is correct, most do agree that the foundation of all explanations must be
food. The availability of food is the driving force in the evolution of
migration patterns. Food abundance can increase reproductive out-
put; lack of food leads to death. A bird that can find more food will
live longer and produce more offspring than one that finds less food.
If by moving from place to place a bird can find more food, migration will evolve.

Migration biologists often evaluate the potential for migration as
a cost-benefit relationship. David Lack, a British ornithologist and
evolutionary biologist, stated that migration will evolve only if the
costs of migration are less than benefits. Cost and benefit are both
measured in mortality and reproduction. If the cost of migration is
great, mortality will be high and reproduction will be low. If the
benefit of migration is great, mortality will be low and reproduction
will be high. It is very similar to running a business; costs must be
kept to a minimum so that benefits (profits) will be high.

We now know that the geographic patterns of migration can
change during relatively short periods of time. Many songbirds no
longer migrate as far south in winter because they can feast at subur-
ban birdfeeders in the north. As a consequence, the migratory habits
of Sharp-shinned Hawks have changed, too. These small woodland
hawks feed on songbirds. When songbirds aggregate in large numbers at feeders, they are easy prey, so this hawk now hunts at feeders.
Some individuals work feeders like a trapline, flying from one to
the next until they surprise and capture their prey. Christmas Bird
Counts in the northeastern United States show that numbers of
Sharp-shinned Hawks have increased in recent years, presumably
because of the increase in overwintering songbirds.

Another hawk that has changed its migratory tendencies is the
Red Kite, a European hawk. This species used to migrate far south
for the winter. With more people, more garbage, and more landfills,
it has abandoned its migration from some areas because it now has

food available throughout the winter. The landfills are magnets for rats and thus for some raptors that feed on both the garbage and the rodents.

To the frustration of duck hunters in the southern United States, the practice of "short-stopping" has abbreviated the migratory flights of some species. Because farmers are leaving crops standing in the northern United States, providing food for ducks and geese, the waterfowl need not migrate as far south.

These examples show how flexible birds are—a theme that will run throughout this book. This very plasticity of migration behavior and ecology is what makes it so difficult to explain bird migration and trace its evolution.

Two

How Scientists Study Migration

BIRD MIGRATION HAS IGNITED THE PASSION AND IMAGINATION OF SCIENtists for hundreds of years. During the centuries we have pondered the migration of birds, we have tried to learn about migration in many ways, using different techniques to answer different questions. Because migration is so difficult to study, researchers have had to overcome many stumbling blocks by trial and error. Good migration research requires lots of work and a blend of the appropriate research design and analysis.

Migration research is constantly changing. New methods are always emerging and old ones are being refined. Graduate students, postdoctoral fellows, and tenured faculty are devising new methods for studying migration. New techniques designed to answer specific questions about migration will bring exciting discoveries.

Overviews of the most widely used methods for studying migration are presented in this chapter. It is impossible to describe these methods without discussing some of the questions that can be answered using them. You may wish to refer to specific methods described in this chapter if you are unsure about a technique mentioned later in the book.

INDIRECT METHODS

Much of what we know about bird migration has been learned by people who weren't actually studying it. Faunal accounts, Christmas

Bird Counts, specimen collections in museums, and even unpublished anecdotes and diaries of birders all provide information about the migration of birds.

Faunal accounts tell us which species migrate and how far they go. Early naturalists who traveled to South America, South Asia, Africa, and other remote parts of the world kept careful notes about what types of birds they saw and when they saw them. For example, the early writings of W. H. Hudson in southern South America reveal that Swainson's Hawks were abundant on the plains of Argentina during the North American winter. Early naturalists' reports gave us our first indication of which species migrated, where they went, and when they traveled. Without this type of information, we would know little about bird migration in general, not to mention the decline in population and changes in migratory routes of certain species.

Old faunal accounts are wonderful reading, but they are not complete. Pick up an issue of a modern ornithological journal or a new book on tropical bird faunas and you will see that new information about migration is still being gathered. An article in a 1990 issue of *Condor* by Floyd Hayes and several others detailed sightings of about thirty species of North American migrants in Paraguay; six of these species had not been seen there before. Articles like this one are filling in gaps in our knowledge of the geographic and seasonal aspects of migration.

Modern faunal accounts are useful, too. Five times a year, *American Birds,* published by the National Audubon Society, provides fine qualitative information, especially regarding birds that are rare or out of their normal geographic range. Most importantly, *American Birds* publishes the Christmas Bird Counts (CBC). Nearly two thousand CBCs are done each year, mostly in North America. Each reports all birds seen within a fifteen-mile radius during a specified time. The information provides a valuable long-term record of bird populations and winter distribution of North American birds. An analysis of ten years of CBC data has been published in *Winter Distributions of North American Birds* (University of Chicago Press). Combined with breeding range maps and other information, CBCs are a vital (and mostly untapped) resource to migration researchers.

Detailed bird records are also kept at the state level by such organizations as the New Jersey Audubon Society, which publishes *Records of New Jersey Birds* four times a year. Also at the state level are breeding bird atlases, published by various nonprofit organizations and state wildlife agencies.

In addition to faunal accounts, the old-time explorers also collected specimens (now called study skins) for museums throughout the world. Although they may smell like mothballs, the skin collections of such wonderful museums as Chicago's Field Museum, Philadelphia's Academy of Natural Science, and the University of Kansas museum are tremendous repositories of data just waiting to be analyzed. There are now several million specimens in museums around the world and the collections are still expanding.

Museum skins are a bit inaccessible, and only limited numbers of skins exist for most species. I traveled to more than thirty museums to find 825 Snowy Owl specimens for a study of age and sex differences in the migration and wintering range.

BANDING, OR RINGING

Although faunal accounts tell us where birds occur during the breeding, migration, and winter seasons, they tell us little about the movements of individual birds. This information can be acquired through banding studies, called "ringing" in Europe.

Banding is a four-part process. First, researchers catch the birds. Then they band and measure them. Next, they release the birds into the wild. Finally, they transfer the information into a data base. Birds are captured with nets or traps. The standard mist net is about 12 meters long and 2.5 meters high and made of thread so fine that a bird cannot see it until it has already become entangled. Once the bird is caught, the researcher places it in a bag or dark container.

Songbirds are often placed in cloth bags with drawstrings that prevent escape and damage to feathers. Banders at Cape May, New Jersey, and elsewhere use darkened cans to hold hawks and owls. This reduces stress and keeps them from struggling, which could injure both hawk and bander.

The next step is to place a numbered aluminum band on the bird's tarsus (the part of the foot that appears to be the ankle). The

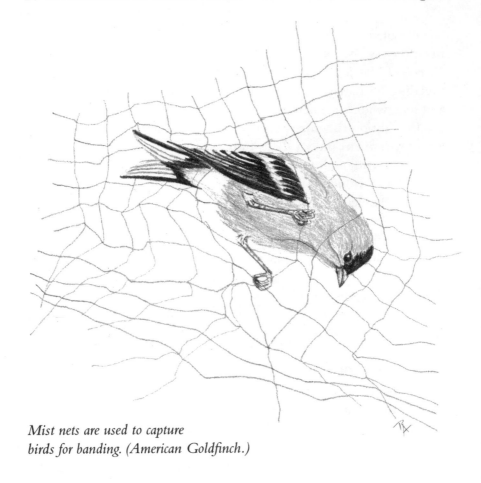

*Mist nets are used to capture
birds for banding. (American Goldfinch.)*

size and type of band is specific to the species, the most basic variety
being a piece of aluminum bent around the tarsus. The ends butt
against each other and are thus called butt-end bands. For birds with
strong beaks that can remove butt-end bands, lock-on bands are used
that have a tab that is folded over onto itself. After a band is in place,
the researcher records the band number, date, time of day, age, sex,
wing chord (distance from the wrist to the end of the longest primary wing feather), mass (or weight), fat condition, and molt. Some
banders also measure tail length, wingspan, hallux (big toenail)
length, and culmen (beak) length.

Once the pertinent information has been recorded, the birds are
released. The banding process, from capture to release, can take as

little as two minutes or as long as two hours. Most birds are banded in less than forty-five minutes, and good banders release birds quickly.

Banding done on the nesting grounds and wintering grounds as well as during migration itself can provide information for migration studies. Banding studies help us piece together migration by providing information on migration pathways between breeding and wintering areas. They also show differences in migration behavior and ecology, such as variation in the seasonal timing or the winter range of age and sex classes of a species.

Bands used in North America come from the U.S. Fish and Wildlife Service's Bird Banding Laboratory. Banders are licensed by USFWS and state agencies and must train for three or four years as apprentices. Records of birds banded in the United States are stored on a BBL computer database. The BBL licenses thousands of banders, distributes millions of bands, curates millions of records, and publishes a bird-banding manual.

Butt-end band

Lock-on band

The aluminum U.S. Fish and Wildlife Service band enables researchers to track the movements of birds. The butt-end band (top) works fine for the Snowy Egret, but Merlins and other birds with strong bills must be fitted with lock-on bands.

In North America long-term, large-scale banding projects are adding significantly to our knowledge of migration. Ongoing studies are now conducted by Point Reyes Bird Observatory (California), Manomet Bird Observatory (Massachusetts), Braddock Bay Raptor Research (New York), Colorado Bird Observatory, Whitefish Bird Observatory (Michigan), Hubbard Brook (Dartmouth College), and Cape May Bird Observatory (New Jersey), among others. Many of those involved in banding are volunteers.

Bird banding has its shortcomings and biases. For every bird recovered a distance from the banding site, perhaps a hundred are never seen again. Before the 1950s the recovery rate for banded hawks was 5 to 10 percent because shooting them was legal. The current rate of recovery in North America is about 1 to 3 percent. In some parts of the world the recovery rate is still rather high. Elliot McClure, the dean of American bird banders, reported that just 4 percent—104 of 2,486—of the Gray-faced Buzzard Eagles banded on Miyako Jima (an island between Japan and the Philippines) were recovered. These birds were banded during migration from north-eastern China, Korea, and Japan into the Philippines. Most of the recoveries were of birds taken in the Philippines for food. There's no way to tell how many more were taken but not reported. Nevertheless, banding data represent a gold mine of information and could be better exploited.

RADAR

Perhaps the most important breakthrough in the study of bird migration was the invention of radar in the early 1940s. Near the end of World War II technicians watched the first radar screens and saw mysterious echoes, which they called angels. Today, some radar technicians still do not know that "angels" are birds and call them AP, for anomalous propagation.

As radar began to be used, the door to migration study opened. Information was gathered faster than it could be analyzed or assimilated. David Lack, one of the great ornithologists and evolutionary biologists of the century, conducted some of the first radar studies in Great Britain, where he "watched" the arrival and departure of

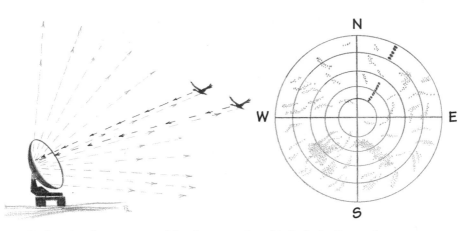

Radar signals are returned by the water in a bird's body. Researchers can easily distinguish between an airplane (the dark blips) and a flock of migrating birds (the so-called angels) on a radar plan position indicator.

migrants in the British Isles. His studies included both nocturnal and diurnal movements of songbirds and shorebirds.

Since Lack's studies, the use of radar for migration research has spread to many parts of the world. New technologies evolved, and scientists quickly realized that they could learn more about bird migration by using these new radars. At least four types of radar have been used to study migration, each of which has its advantages and disadvantages: airport surveillance radar (ASR), weather surveillance radar (WSR), tracking radar, and marine surveillance radar. Radar relies on microwaves that are reflected off an object from a microwave transmitter. What the radar "sees" is the radar-reflective material within a body. In aircraft, metal reflects microwaves; in birds and even insects, water is the reflector.

Radar is basically a range-finding device. The difference among radars is in power and beam shape. Marine and airport surveillance radars rely on a fan-shaped beam that is about 23 degrees in height above the horizon and about 2 degrees in horizontal width. Weather and tracking radars have a conical beam of only ½ of 1 degree. Airport and marine radars cannot measure altitude. (You may be surprised that airport radar does not give air-traffic controllers information on altitude. They determine whether two planes are flying at the same altitude via a transponder that sends the aircraft's identification number and altitude directly to a radar monitor.)

Whereas most radars are used to examine the movement of large numbers of birds over several hundred square kilometers, tracking radar locks on to individual migrants and follows them until they are out of range. The position of each bird is recorded every few seconds, and its speed, altitude, direction, and mode of flight (soaring or flapping) are measured with precision. During daylight, the species of the bird being tracked can often be identified. At least one biologist has fixed a powerful spotlight on the radar antenna to identify nocturnal migrants. Despite its advantages, tracking radar has been exploited by few researchers.

Radar answers more questions about the actual flight behavior of migrants than any other technique. When during the day or night do birds migrate? How many hours a day or night do migrants fly? Do migrants cease migration when it rains or when the wind direction changes? How high do birds fly? How fast do birds fly? In what direction do migrants fly? How many migrants are aloft? Are birds migrating in flocks?

Although radar is a wonderful and versatile tool, it has its shortcomings. It cannot, for example, identify the targets being tracked, and it is effective in only a small area. Without the bits and snatches of information radar does provide, however, we would know very little about the flight behavior of migrating birds.

RADIOTELEMETRY AND SPECIAL MARKING
Since the advent of electronic miniaturization, we have had the technology to let birds tell us where they are and what they are doing. Radiotelemetry is the technique of putting radiotransmitters on birds so that their movements and activities can be monitored from a distance.

Transmitters weighing less than 3 percent of a bird's body weight are attached to a bird's back with a harness or to a tail feather using string and glue. Usually, birds adjust to them rapidly. The transmitter sends out a signal every so many seconds. Most transmitters are powered by batteries, although a few are solar powered. Solar cells are

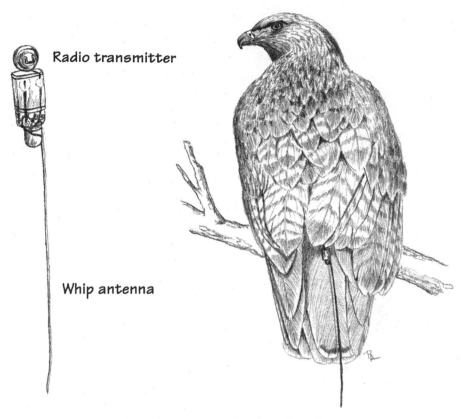

Radio transmitter

Whip antenna

A radiotransmitter with a whip antenna, placed on the tail, permits researchers to follow a bird's migration for hundreds of miles. (Red-tailed Hawk.)

heavier but transmit longer. If a researcher wishes to follow a bird for days or weeks during migration, a battery pack is preferable. For longer distances and longer time periods (months or years), larger batteries or solar-powered packs are required. These can be heavy and are now used only on large birds, like Bald Eagles.

Once a transmitter is attached to a bird, the researcher follows it from an automobile or airplane fitted with an antenna to receive the transmitted signal. This is not easy. Al Harmata, studying Bald Eagle movements in the Rocky Mountains and Great Plains, tells animated tales of trying to follow birds for hundreds of miles through virtually trackless regions. He has been successful through dogged hard work

A streamer can be seen from a distance of several hundred yards. (Ferruginous Hawk.)

and innovative techniques. Another researcher tracked Red-tailed Hawks for long distances along the ridges and valleys of eastern Pennsylvania near Hawk Mountain. One migrant was followed to its wintering site, where its movements were monitored until spring.

Now that smaller and more powerful transmitters are available, we can track birds anywhere. In the past few years scientists have even attempted to follow radio-tagged Bald Eagles and Tundra Swans by satellite.

Data gathered with radiotelemetry are more detailed than those yielded by other modes of studying migration. Because individuals can be followed throughout the day on successive days, researchers can learn behavioral sequences—how migrants change their behavior according to the weather, terrain, and geographic location. It is even possible to follow birds from their breeding site to their wintering site and back again. Because few birds can be tracked at one time, radiotelemetry studies are necessarily limited to small samples.

As with radiotelemetry, special marking projects attempt to follow individuals or small groups of migrating birds. In this case, direct visual contact must be made or the data are invalid. Tail streamers, sometimes made of electrical tape, have been used at Cape May and Hawk Mountain to determine how far birds move and where they move with respect to topography and weather. Using different colors and shapes on different days, researchers at Cape May studied the behavior of Sharp-shinned and Red-tailed hawks attempting to cross the Delaware Bay. Tail streamers are effective, but they are difficult to see at distances greater than 200 meters (650 feet), and birds can preen them off.

Patagial tags—colored plastic tags about 8 centimeters (3 inches) square imprinted with a number or letter—are probably the best

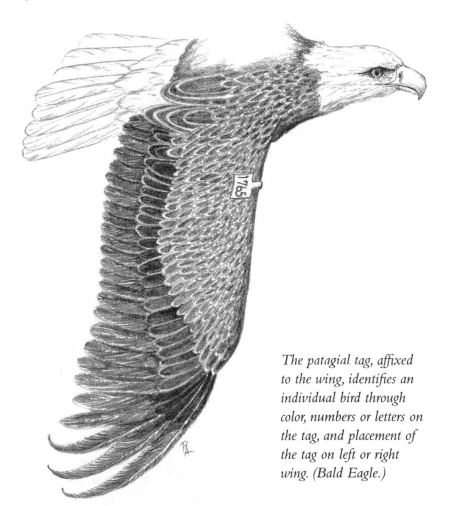

The patagial tag, affixed to the wing, identifies an individual bird through color, numbers or letters on the tag, and placement of the tag on left or right wing. (Bald Eagle.)

types of markers to use with large birds. They are pop-riveted through the patagium, an area of skin between the wrist and the elbow. They are most visible from above and often disappear when a bird is perched. The numbers on large patagial tags, such as those used for eagles and hawks, can be read at several hundred yards. A unique combination of color, wing (right or left), and number on the tag identifies the individual. Although migration researchers have not used patagial tags, birds marked in this way for other purposes have been seen far from the marking site, showing that the birds have migrated.

Other color marking methods are used in limited studies. For example, waterfowl biologists sometimes use numbered neck rings to mark individual Canada Geese and numbered nasal saddles to mark ducks. The numbers can be read with relative ease from several hundred feet away.

Colored bands placed on a bird's tarsus are ideal for studying long-distance movements and stopover timing. Birds banded in South America, for example, have been resighted along the Delaware Bay of New Jersey. For nearly a decade, Brian Harrington of the Manomet Bird Observatory, in Massachusetts, has placed colored tarsal bands made of plastic on Red Knots. Using this method, Harrington has examined such aspects of migration as fidelity to stopover sites, duration of stopover by individuals, and longevity.

VISUAL TECHNIQUES

The human eye is one of the best tools for studying migration. For centuries all that we knew about migration was the result of direct observation of the seasonal movements of birds. The observation of migrants can reveal much about their behavior and ecology, such as seasonal and daily timing of migration, and habitat use.

Visual studies have also helped us learn about the orientation and navigation of migrants. Migration counts can be used in concert with compasses to determine the direction of migration and how a bird responds to topographic and weather changes. Moon watching and the use of ceilometers are other visual techniques that have been used to determine the direction of migratory flight and the number

By watching the moon, researchers can determine the number and direction of birds aloft. As migrants fly across the bright background of the moon, they are readily visible through a scope or binoculars. Clockface times or a compass rose helps determine direction.

of migrants aloft. These methods are most effective with songbirds that migrate at night. By watching the moon with a telescope and recording the direction of birds as they cross the moon, scientists from Louisiana State University did some of the pioneering work in bird migration. Direction is ascertained by viewing the moon as a clock face and noting the "hours" through which a bird passes. When the moon is directly overhead, the observer orients his head to the north; a bird passing from twelve o'clock to six o'clock is migrating due south. When the moon is not directly overhead, however, determining migration direction is more complex.

Using a ceilometer—a bright, narrow-beamed light shone straight up into the sky at night—is easier than watching the moon.

Looking up a ceilometer beam, the researcher can count migrating birds and note their direction as they fly through the bright light several hundred feet above.

The researcher lies on his back with his head pointing north and looks up the beam through a spotting scope or high-powered binoculars. As birds pass through the ceilometer beam, their direction is given as clockface or compass coordinates.

Migrating hawks are counted during daylight at hundreds of sites around the world by thousands of hawk-watchers. The thousand or so members of the Hawk Migration Association of North America (HMANA) count migrants as they pass, recording the number of each species in half-hour intervals. Hawks have been systematically counted at Hawk Mountain Sanctuary in Pennsylvania since the 1930s. These counts reflect the upward and downward swings of the populations of many species of raptors and are a useful and cost-effective means of monitoring hawk populations over decades.

Most other birds are not counted as frequently as hawks, but enthusiastic birders count songbirds in such places as Cape May and Falsterbo, Sweden. At Cape May, the counts have been used to study the morning flight of songbirds that migrate at night. The Whitefish Point Bird Observatory in Michigan and the Cape May Bird Observatory conduct waterbird migration counts every year. In some years at Cape May, more than a half-million seabirds are sighted (50,000 Red-throated Loons, 3,000 Common Loons, 200,000 scoters of three species, 25,000 Northern Gannets, 150,000 Double-crested Cormorants, and many others). The information has shown that oil or chemical spills at certain times of the year could jeopardize the populations of these species.

Although visual observations can be a cost-effective means of learning about migration, the visual technique is not without biases. How do we observe birds at night or in the twilight of dawn and dusk? How can we count or study the behavior of birds that fly at several hundred feet (one hundred meters) above the ground? Is it possible to observe migrating seabirds that may be a mile (one to two kilometers) offshore? For now, visual observations are limited to low-altitude flights of birds that occur over or close to land during daytime. These constraints eliminate a major portion of migration—the birds that fly at night, over the sea, or at high altitudes.

LABORATORY RESEARCH

The physiological and neural mechanisms that control a migrant's behavior can be studied in migration laboratories that are designed to duplicate the migratory environment. Birds rarely fly in these labs. Instead, a researcher creates a controlled environment that simulates one or more aspects of migration, then manipulates it experimentally.

Three aspects of migration are studied most often in the laboratory: orientation and navigation, biological rhythms related to migration schedule, and the physiology and endocrinology of fat deposition and migratory readiness. To study orientation, researchers place birds in Emlen funnels, or orientation cages, and expose them to the night sky, a planetarium sky, an altered magnetic field, polarized light, or some other potential orientation cue to determine whether they are capable of using it. Their movements are then monitored to see whether they hop in a particular direction.

To study migratory readiness, researchers use activity cages in which birds are exposed to such environmental cues as length of daylight period or temperature. The amount of hopping is a measure of migratory activity or migratory readiness. Birds that hop a lot at night are ready to migrate.

In the controlled environment of the laboratory, researchers can address questions about migration that cannot be adequately examined in the field. The ability to manipulate the environment is paramount to doing experiments. Since we cannot control the outdoor environment, we must attempt to establish indoor conditions, or paradigms, that allow us to manipulate one or two aspects of the migratory environment.

Today's researchers have incorporated more and more natural variables into their research design. By raising birds in controlled environments, sometimes outside, they are able to study the development of different aspects of migratory behavior. This allows them to use natural cues, such as the setting sun or changing day length, while controlling other cues experimentally.

More recently, laboratory experimentation has begun to involve the use of captive or controlled breeding. By crossbreeding populations of birds with different migratory tendencies, researchers have determined that there is a genetic component to migratory tendency. This sort of research is answering some of the most fundamental questions about migration and is very promising for future research.

Just as there are trends in clothing and fashion, there are also trends in research. From the late 1940s into the mid-1970s observational research was considered the normal way for migration biologists to investigate a phenomenon. That is, they went out and observed nature and measured it as precisely as possible. Using their data, they either tested hypotheses or made post hoc conclusions about what animals were doing.

During the late 1970s and early 1980s experimental studies in migration biology were in favor, and observational research was considered passé. Researchers considered observational studies flawed because they lacked the control of experimental research, and agency funding favored experiments over observation.

Unfortunately, if researchers were to use the experimental approach to the exclusion of observable data (or vice versa), we would know little about migration. I feel that the best means of learning about migration is through observational studies or field trials involving some natural experimentation. By *natural experiment* I mean that researchers study a phenomenon with a variety of environmental conditions or situations, such as wind, cloud cover, presence or absence of other individuals, or season. Although true control is absent in natural experiments, these environmental situations are analogous to treatments in laboratory experiments. As the environment changes, a bird's behavior or physiology is monitored.

Controlled laboratory experiments do have their place. Experimentation with controls is needed, especially to learn about the mechanisms that govern the behavior of migrants. Observational and experimental studies are complementary, with each contributing to our knowledge of migration and together providing us with pieces of the migration puzzle.

THREE

The Basics of Bird Flight

SOMEBODY ONCE TOLD ME THAT ANALYZING AND STUDYING AN ANIMAL demystify it, making it less interesting and less awe inspiring. Nothing could be further from the truth. The more I study flight and migration, the more I appreciate birds. Engineers have tried for more than a century to perfect flying machines. But is there any aircraft designed by man that can land in a tree, take off in the forest, fly through the woods, dive into the ocean and take off again, land on a cliff, or fly just inches from ocean swells?

Leonardo da Vinci's designs of flying machines reveal enormous

Powered flight: Canada Goose

insight into the complexities of flight. Flight is indeed complex, and it is unfortunate that terms like aerodynamic performance, flight energetics, fat metabolism, flight morphology, glide ratio, aspect ratio, wing loading, lift, and drag conjure visions of mind-boggling mathematical equations. Yet flight dynamics is the foundation of migration studies because flight is the single most outstanding feature of birds and their migration. Understanding flight is integral to understanding migratory behavior and ecology.

TYPES OF FLIGHT

There are at least five types of flight birds use during migration: powered, bounding, undulating (also called flap and glide), partially powered gliding, and gliding. Though these are described as distinct categories, in some cases they intergrade. In addition, some species are capable of several types of flight, depending on weather and other circumstances.

Powered flight, characterized by continuous flapping, is used by sandpipers, ducks, geese, rails, hummingbirds, and some others. The wings move constantly except for brief moments during landing, when the wings stop flapping to glide or parachute downward. Powered flight is usually marked by a level course through the air.

Some of the smallest birds, such as warblers, vireos, small woodpeckers, thrushes, orioles, robins, and tanagers, use *bounding,* a type of

Powered flight means continuous flapping.

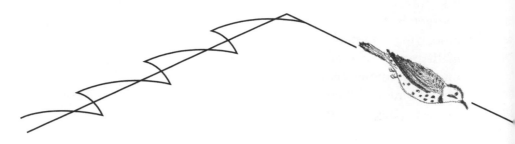

Bounding flight: Northern Flicker

powered flight. These birds flap their wings in short bursts during which they gain altitude; they then descend steeply, with their wings folded against the body. These birds are constantly climbing and descending, although the overall flight path is level.

Undulating is another form of powered flight with a nonlevel flight path. The wings are flapped in bursts, as in bounding, but instead of bringing the wings in to the body between bursts, the bird holds them out as in gliding. Crows, some larger woodpeckers, some hawks, cormorants, ibis, petrels, herons, and egrets are among the

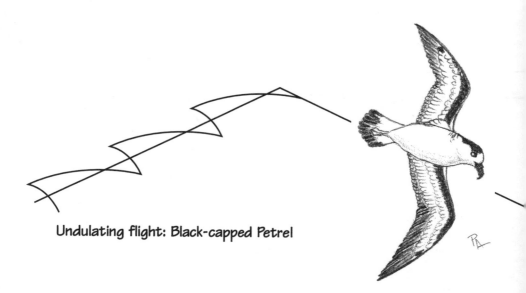

Undulating flight: Black-capped Petrel

Most songbirds employ a bounding flight:
bursts of flapping, during which the bird gains altitude,
followed by a dive with the wings close to the body.

birds that use this form of flight. Undulating flight intergrades with the partially powered gliding.

A bird using a *partially powered glide* alternates between flapping its wings and holding them still in an extended position. During the flapping sequence the bird need not gain altitude. Small hawks, such as the Sharp-shinned Hawk, often use a partially powered glide when flying between thermals, perhaps because it provides extra

In undulating flight,
the bird flaps its wings several times to
gain altitude, then stretches out its wings for a long glide.

thrust to increase speed or extend the glide. Cranes, swallows, swifts, pelicans, gannets, cormorants, ibis, petrels, shearwaters, and others use partially powered glides when they are not using intermittent powered or gliding flight. Interestingly, many of these species can use continuous flapping (powered) or pure gliding flight as well.

Gliding is flight with fixed wings and no flapping. During gliding flight a bird loses altitude unless a current of air is rising faster than the bird is sinking. Soaring is gliding at slow speeds in circles, usually in thermal updrafts. Watch a hawk circling in an updraft or

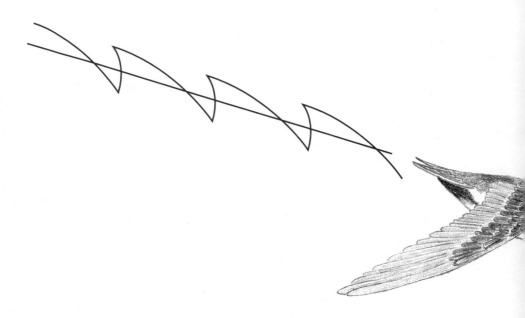

Partially powered flight: White-throated Swift

gliding in one direction: the only difference between soaring and gliding is that soaring entails circling, whereas gliding is in a relatively straight line. The types of birds that glide include pelicans, gannets, petrels, albatrosses, cranes, hawks, swallows, and swifts. All of these birds use powered flight to take off or when updrafts are not available.

To hone your observational skills, identify which types of flight are used by different birds. The next time you see a bird in flight, observe it carefully and note how it flies. If you see a bird change its flight pattern, consider why this happened. Although you may have more questions than when you started, you will gain a greater appreciation for flight. Leonardo also learned by watching birds.

A partially powered flier
combines gliding and flapping.

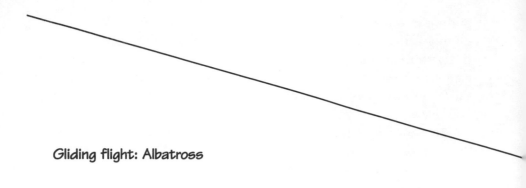

Gliding flight: Albatross

FLIGHT STRUCTURE

To describe a bird's flight capability, we need to consider mass, the wing, and the tail. Mass often is incorrectly called weight. Wing considerations include wingspan (tip to tip), wing area (surface area), and wing-tip shape. Tail length and shape also determine how a bird performs in flight.

It's important to compare birds of similar size, since flight performance varies with size. In general, heavy birds, such as geese and ducks, fly faster than light birds, such as warblers and flycatchers. Birds with long, pointed wings fly faster and live in open country or over the sea; birds with short, rounded wings fly more slowly and live in forested areas. The long, narrow wings, called high-aspect-ratio wings, of albatrosses, petrels, shearwaters, and gulls enable them to glide rapidly over the water or engage in long-distance powered flight; broad, rounded wings are not as efficient for powered or gliding flight. Birds that inhabit forests have short, rounded wings for maneuvering in tight quarters.

There are other examples of wing shape correlating with migration distance, although few biologists have made an effort to investigate this relationship—perhaps because the issues are so complicated. The evolutionary control of wing shape of any particular species is a

With gliding flight comes a continuous loss of altitude; there is no flapping.

function of genetic history as well as migration distance, habitat use, and foraging method. None of these factors act independently, of course, and a bird's wing structure is usually a compromise of many competing selective pressures. Researchers will need to devise new means of analyzing wing structure and selective pressures.

The Sanderling is a typical shorebird, with long pointed wings suitable for fast flight over open water and beaches.

| CASE STUDY | "Shorebirds" That Live in the Forest Have Short Wings. |

SHOREBIRDS PROVIDE AN EXCELLENT EXAMPLE OF HOW A BIRD'S WING shape is related to habitat. Most shorebirds have long, pointed wings that permit fast and powerful flight. A few shorebirds, however, have short wings and rounded wing tips. The American Woodcock (also called Timberdoodle) is an aberrant shorebird that lives in the forest. Its short wings with rounded tips promote maneuverability in the forest but are not suited for long-distance migration or fast flight. Another feature that makes this bird distinct from other shorebirds is the absence of stiff flight feathers—the primaries at the ends of the wings. Most woodland species have softer, more pliant flight feathers than do birds of open country: soft feathers are less likely to suffer damage from impact with branches, and stiff feathers promote fast flight in open spaces. These forest birds have adaptations that make them more maneuverable than open-country birds of the same size. ∎

The American Woodcock, too, is a shorebird, but it has adapted to maneuvering through its woodland habitat with shorter, more rounded wings.

CASE STUDY	*Hawks' Wings Differ with Migration Distance.*

THE SHARP-SHINNED HAWK OF NORTH AMERICA AND THE GRAY FROG Hawk (also called Chinese Goshawk) from Southeast Asia are closely related (both are in the genus *Accipiter*) and about the same size: males weigh about 100 grams, and females, 170 grams. Sharp-shinned Hawks, which have a wingspan of 15 to 18 inches (381 to 457 mm), are medium-distance migrants over much of their range, and they rarely cross large bodies of water. The Gray Frog Hawk, on the other hand, migrates farther and makes water crossings of 300 miles (480 kilometers) between China and the islands of Southeast Asia. The difference in migratory distance and water-crossing tendency correlates with differences in wing shape. The wings of the Gray Frog Hawk are much longer than those of the Sharp-shinned Hawk; they are more pointed as well. These wings enable Gray Frog Hawks to fly longer and faster than Sharp-shinned Hawks. ■

The primary feathers in the tips of raptors' wings are flexible, turning upward in slow glides to provide an aerodynamic advantage. (Golden Eagle.)

CASE STUDY	*Warbler Wings Vary with Foraging Behavior and Migration Distance.*

MOST NORTH AMERICAN WOOD WARBLERS FORAGE IN FORESTED OR shrubby habitats. If foraging were the only selective force that acts upon the evolution of birds' flight morphology, we might expect all warblers with the same foraging habits to have wings of the same shape. This is not the case, however. Meticulous studies of the structure of warbler wings have revealed that foraging behavior is the most important selective factor influencing wing shape, with migration distance being a secondary factor. Cerulean, Bay-breasted, and Blackpoll warblers have long, pointed wings because they fly a lot while foraging in the treetops and because they migrate long distances. In Europe, the Wood Warbler (more closely related to North American kinglets than to wood warblers) also has long, pointed wings and is both an arboreal forager and a long-distance migrant. Ovenbirds and Connecticut Warblers, which forage on or near the ground, have long, pointed wings because they are long-distance migrants. Common Yellowthroats and Mourning Warblers have shorter, more rounded wing tips. They forage in thick brush and do not migrate as far as some other warblers. ∎

*Vortices form because
air flows faster over the top
of the feathers. By separating the
primaries at the wingtip, a soaring bird
can break a big, strong vortex into several
small, weak vortices, thereby reducing overall drag.*

Watch a hawk, eagle, pelican, or crane soar upward in a thermal. The primary feathers flex upward at the tip and are separated as if the wing had fingers. These openings, called slots, are formed by indentations (called emarginations) of the trailing and leading edges of the feathers closest to the wing tip. Slotting is found most often on wings that have rounded tips. On slotted wings, the third or fourth feather back from the wing tip is the longest; on a pointed wing, without slots, the ninth or tenth primary (nearest the tip) is the longest. During slow gliding or soaring flight, the slotted feathers at the wing tips are bent upward. In species like Turkey Vultures or eagles, the wing tips are flexible and turn upward dramatically.

The flexibility (called aeroelasticity) and slotting may reduce drag. Air moves faster over the top of the convex structure of the wing, generating lift. As lift is generated, a vortex forms behind and at the end of the wing. As a bird moves, it must pull this vortex with it. Wing-tip slots create many smaller vortices, one at each feather tip, reducing overall drag. Birds with pointed wings have smaller wing-tip vortices than birds with wide, rounded wings. There are, then, at least two adaptive strategies to reduce drag.

A bird's tail, like its wings, is an airfoil and generates both lift and drag. A bird changes the relative proportions of these two forces by changing the way it holds its tail as it flies. A bird that is landing opens its tail to provide more lift at slower speeds and pushes its tail downward to increase drag and slow down. A bird that is turning or landing can open its tail so that it acts as a rudder or air brake. And a bird that is soaring in a thermal can open its tail so that it climbs faster. The same bird closes its tail when flying between thermals so that it generates less drag.

CASE STUDY	*Comparing the Tails of Three Hawks.*

A COMPARISON OF THREE HAWKS OF SIMILAR SIZE SHOWS HOW DIFFERent tails can be and how this difference relates to habitat and differences in hunting behavior. Northern Goshawks, Peregrine Falcons, and Red-shouldered Hawks are predators weighing 500 to 1,000 grams. Northern Goshawks have very long tails that enable them to stop and turn rapidly in the forest, where they hunt birds and mammals. During migration they use a combination of gliding and intermittent gliding flight. Red-shouldered Hawks live in the forest or at the forest edge, where they hunt small mammals, amphibians, reptiles, and birds. Although they hunt from perches much of the time, they also soar over the forest or over open fields while looking for prey. In migration they use gliding and soaring flight almost exclusively. The tail is not nearly so long as the goshawk's because the Red-shouldered Hawk rarely pursues its prey through the forest. Peregrines also have shorter tails than goshawks because their hunting mode is very different. They hunt in open tundra, marshes, savannahs, farm fields, ocean, and beaches mostly by soaring with an occasional dive at prey, or by powered flight. Unlike goshawks, Peregrine Falcons never chase their prey into or through the forest. During migration they either glide from thermal to thermal or use powered flight. When soaring, all of these species open their tails wide, presenting more surface area that yields more lift at slower speeds. By doing this they can remain in the smallest thermals or in the area of a thermal with the strongest updrafts. ■

As with wing structure, many competing selective forces determine tail size and shape. Perhaps the most extreme example is a woodpecker's tail, which is adapted for use as a stabilizing lever while the bird is foraging on a tree trunk. Its stiff, pointed feathers are not efficient airfoils, and the tail is hardly used in flight. For the woodpecker tail, foraging behavior seems to be the strongest selective pressure.

GLIDING PERFORMANCE

The best measure of the flight performance of a gliding bird is its glide ratio—forward distance divided by the distance it sinks. This is usually expressed as a ratio of forward speed to sinking speed. The glide ratio of a bird is not fixed; that is, a bird can change the way it holds its wings so that it can fly faster or slower. At the best glide speed, a bird achieves the best glide ratio at an airspeed that is just above the slowest speed it can maintain without stalling. As it flies faster, its sink rate increases quickly, so the bird realizes lower glide ratios. A Broad-winged Hawk is capable of realizing maximum glide ratios of about 11:1, but during interthermal glides in migration the glide ratios are reduced to 7 or 8. To fly faster (and, of course, sink faster) these and other soaring birds pull in their wings so that less surface area is exposed and wingspan is reduced.

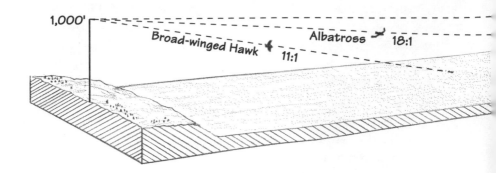

To see nearly the entire range of gliding capabilities, let's compare sailplanes, monarch butterflies, and various species of birds. Sailplanes always have much higher glide ratios than birds and insects. A high-performance sailplane can have a glide ratio in excess of 40. This means that from a mile high (assuming no wind), it can glide for 40 miles without hitting the ground. A monarch butterfly's best glide is 3: from a foot-high blossom it could glide 3 feet. A pigeon's glide ratio is 4 or 5. Even such gliding migrants as Broadwinged Hawks, Ospreys, large vultures, and albatrosses cannot compete with sailplanes when it comes to glide ratio. The best glide ratio for hawks in the middle to larger size range is between 10 and 13: from an altitude of 1 mile (1.6 kilometers), which is a bit higher than they usually fly but not out of the migration range, these migrants could realize glides of 10 to 13 miles (16 to 20.8 kilometers). Large vultures, eagles, and albatrosses have glide ratios in the range of 14 to 18, sometimes higher. During migration they rarely use the best glide ratio. Instead, they travel at faster airspeeds, which reduces their glide ratio. Actual migration glide ratios are in the 7 to 12 range for birds in still air. With a tailwind these migrants can realize over-the-ground glide ratios of 20 or better. With a headwind they may realize a glide ratio of only 5.

NATURALLY SELECTED FLIGHT STRUCTURES
Foraging, predator avoidance, habitat, migration: these selective pressures work together on the gene pool of a species to shape the evolutionary history of a species, making it what we see today. It is fairly

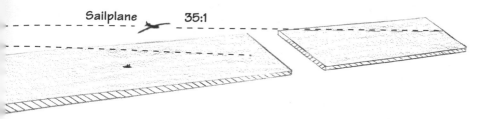

An albatross can glide eighteen
feet while losing only one foot of altitude; a hawk's
gliding performance is not quite so spectacular, but still impressive.

easy to understand how habitat, predator avoidance, and foraging might shape flight morphology, but the influence of migration is not so apparent. The farther a species migrates, the more likely migration is to have shaped its flight structures. As birds fly longer distances, they face more risks and, presumably, more intense selective pressures. This is especially the case for species that must contend with ecological barriers, such as oceans.

To say that migration has shaped the wing structure of a given species is probably correct, but it is almost impossible to prove. The best evidence that migration is an evolutionary force on wing shape is comparisons of closely related species with different migratory behavior. If wing-shape differences in two closely related species are correlated with differences in migration distance, for example, we may infer that migration has played a role in natural selection.

FUEL FOR FLIGHT

Flying is a costly form of transportation. The distance a bird can travel on a given amount of energy is related to the type of flight it uses and to its body structure. Powered flight uses more energy than gliding flight. The three forms of powered flight probably use about the same amount of energy, although this has never been investigated. The reason some birds use bounding or undulating flight is complex; for more information, see the suggested readings.

A direct comparison of the energy needed for gliding versus powered flight should be made only for birds of the same size and shape. As birds get larger, the cost of flight increases faster than the mass. Energy required for flight increases as a power function, about 1.17, of mass. This nonlinear relation is called scaling. That is, larger birds must exert disproportionately more energy than smaller birds. This may be why so many large raptors and other large birds are gliders.

To fly long distances, as during migration, a bird must carry lots of fuel. Fat is the currency of migration because it provides the greatest amount of energy per unit of weight. The more fat a bird has, within certain bounds, the farther it can fly. Fat is indispensable. Without fat a migrant cannot fly far or survive long periods of inclement weather.

The deposition of fat probably evolved not as an adaptation specifically for migration but as a way to survive a food scarcity or cold, rainy, or snowy weather, which requires greater energy. Snowy Owls and other birds in northern climates have massive fat deposits that allow them to weather storms by fasting for several days.

As migration evolved, fat deposits helped migratory birds survive stopovers in inhospitable places or during harsh weather. Migration probably became a selective force as migratory flights became longer. With this change came larger fat deposits and a physiological system that could mobilize and metabolize, "burn," fat in the body rapidly so that it could be used for flight.

How much energy is in 1 gram of fat? A Worm-eating Warbler weighs about 15 grams and can fly more than 125 miles (200 kilometers) on 1 gram of fat. Larger birds, such as shorebirds, fly shorter distances on a gram of fat because flight is more costly for them.

Birds deposit body fat by eating more—by becoming hyperphagic. The bird eats almost constantly and converts the excess food to fat. Birds do this rapidly, gaining 1 to 10 percent or more of body weight per day. This fat must be deposited in places where it will not get in the way and where it can be used during flight. Most birds deposit fat around internal organs, such as the heart and liver, in the lower abdomen, and in the furculum (above the wishbone, just below the throat). Creamy white or yellowish subcutaneous fat deposits can be seen through the skin of songbirds, small hawks, and shorebirds. When birds are extremely fat, the deposits spill over onto the breast and up under the wings.

The gunners who once shot birds like Eskimo Curlews often found these birds obese. Some birds, upon being shot, would nearly burst because their skin was so tightly stretched over such large fat deposits. Fat birds are less maneuverable and cannot accelerate as fast as lean birds and are thus more subject to predation. Certainly fat was a disadvantage for the curlews, which made themselves attractive targets for market hunters because of it.

Shorebirds, according to researchers, seem to deposit the largest migratory fat stores, with the average being 66 percent (for seventeen species examined). The range was 50 percent to nearly 100 percent, which means that some birds double their lean weight. Songbirds, especially those that fly over the Sahara Desert and the Mediterranean Sea, cross the Gulf of Mexico, or fly over portions of the western Atlantic Ocean, can put on 40 to 70 percent of their body weight in fat (the average for sixty species is 50 percent). Those shorebirds and songbirds mentioned above all migrate from the northern temperate or arctic regions to the tropics; songbirds that migrate shorter distances, usually staying in the temperate zone, gain less than 20 to 40 percent of body weight in fat, with considerable variation among species. Hawks rarely deposit more than about 15 percent of their body weight in fat. American Kestrels on wintering territories have only 5 to 8 percent of their weight as fat. Visual fat deposits are evident on migrating kestrels, Sharp-shinned Hawks, and Merlins, but the deposits do not get as large as those on songbirds or shorebirds. Merlins may have larger fat stores because they migrate longer distances and cross large bodies of water.

Some species deposit migratory fat and gain weight more quickly than others. In general, the larger the bird, the more slowly it gains weight. Although a duck or a goose may deposit more weight on a given day than a small shorebird or songbird, the percentage of body weight is smaller for the larger bird. Songbirds and shorebirds that are long-distance migrants may get fat faster than those that are middle-distance, short-distance, or irruptive migrants. The shorter the migration distance, the slower the rate of weight gain. It seems that through natural selection, long-distance migrants are better adapted to rapidly gaining weight, through physiological and behavioral mechanisms.

Migratory hummingbirds having fat-free weights of less than 5 grams have maximum fat deposition rates of about 10 percent per day. Both North American wood warblers and Old World warblers weighing 10 to 20 grams gain weight more slowly, averaging 3 to 8 percent of their body weight per day. Larger yet, shorebirds in the 100-gram range gain between 2 and 5 percent per day. Finally, birds as large as Brant (1,000 grams) and Canada Geese (3,000 grams), deposit only 1 to 2 percent of their body weight in fat per day. Thus, larger birds must make longer stopovers to gain the same percentage of body weight as smaller birds, and the rate of weight gain changes as migrants acquire migratory fat. A fat bird cannot gain weight as rapidly as a lean bird.

As a migrant flies, it first uses sugars available in the blood and liver. These last for only a short time, and then the bird resorts to fat. Most migration is fueled by fat, but if the bird has depleted its fat deposits, it resorts to burning the protein in its muscles. The breast muscle becomes smaller, the bird flies slower, and eventually it dies. Birds that have metabolized all of their fat stores and even their own muscles are said to have "hatchet-keel," a condition in which the breastbone is jutting out. So when fat deposits are depleted, stop- overs are necessary.

Up in the Air

UNDERSTANDING THE MEDIUM THROUGH WHICH BIRDS FLY IS CRUCIAL to understanding migration. Look out the window and think about how birds fly through the air. The air is forever changing: the atmosphere is never still, just as the weather is never constant. The vertical and horizontal movements of air currents affect the way birds fly, the progress they make, and how much energy they require for flight.

There are two things we need to consider to help us understand how birds are affected when migrating through the air: weather and atmospheric structure. Weather is that aspect of meteorology with which we are most familiar—rain, snow, temperature, wind, fog, and humidity. Atmospheric structure is a result of the weather and includes vertical movement of air, gust structure, temperature gradients above the ground, wind gradients, and wind shear. All these factors have shaped many aspects of the biology of birds—wing and bone structure, musculature, body shape, feathers, physiology, behavior, and not least, migration.

WEATHER

When meteorologists forecast the weather for the week ahead, they often refer to a weather map that shows the location of warm and cold fronts, or systems. Fronts are often associated with major weather changes.

A high-pressure cell is an area of expanding air that can be hundreds to more than a thousand miles in diameter. Inside the high-pressure region the air rotates clockwise. Near the east (or front) and north (or top) sides of a moving high-pressure area, winds blow from the west or northwest. In eastern North America high-pressure cells move from west to east or northwest to southeast. On rare occasions, these cells move from north to south, bringing extremely cold, polar air. The latter are sometimes called polar fronts.

The boundary between two high-pressure cells is the area commonly called a front. It usually includes a low-pressure area, or trough. In a low-pressure area, the air rotates counterclockwise, as in a cyclone or hurricane. In the northeastern United States a low-pressure area often brings winds from an easterly quadrant, with accompanying humidity and precipitation.

Although day-to-day weather is controlled by the movement of high-pressure cells and the low-pressure areas (the fronts) between them, the frequency of fronts and the pattern of their movement (or lack of movement) are correlated with season and geographic area. In northeastern North America the passage of cold fronts is very predictable and accounts for the prevailing westerly winds from September to March, and even into April.

In autumn in northeastern North America a cold front is accompanied by a change of wind, usually from southeast or south to north or west, a change in air temperature from warm to cold, and a change in sky cover from clear or light clouds to very cloudy or complete cloud cover. Frequently, rain or snow is associated with the front. The air behind the cold front, near the leading edge of a high-pressure cell, is characterized by clear skies with or without cumulus clouds (once the front has "cleared" or moved by), drier conditions, and brisk, cool, westerly breezes.

Look at the two weather maps that are typical for autumn and spring in eastern North America. One map is for a late-September day, showing a cold front over Pennsylvania, West Virginia, and Ontario. Wind direction is indicated by arrows, and the area under the cold front is experiencing rain. This is the low-pressure area between two high-pressure cells. The westerly winds behind (west of) the cold front are dry and cool. With the passing of this front, temperatures will drop 10 to 20 degrees Fahrenheit and skies will become clear or somewhat cloudy, and visibility will be almost unlimited. Clouds in the high-pressure area will most likely be fair-weather cumulus; higher, more wispy altocumulus clouds will be evident toward the rear (west side) of the high-pressure zone. If the cold front is strong enough, it will push through to the Atlantic coast, bringing some precipitation and even a thunderstorm or two. Fronts that continue offshore usually dissipate after mixing with the warm air of the ocean. These fronts can also stall anywhere along their west-east or north-south track, producing several days of rain or snow.

In the southeastern United States, below 30 to 35 degrees north latitude, the movement of cold fronts is less predictable. As these fronts move farther south or southeast they lose power and often stall, causing rain and poor weather, sometimes for several days. At some times of year, high-pressure cells become relatively stationary, and the weather changes little for several days or even weeks. In the southeastern United States from March through May a high-pressure cell called a Bermuda high may settle over the western Atlantic Ocean, producing strong southerly or southeasterly winds on the rear, west side of the high-pressure cell.

The other map shows a Bermuda High in mid-April. The approximate center of the high over the western Atlantic Ocean is not far from Bermuda. Winds at this time over the southeastern United States and the Gulf of Mexico are from the south at 10 to 20 miles per hour. This quasi-stable pattern can remain in one place for several days, unlike a cold front, which often blasts through an area.

The direction of prevailing winds is determined by the passage of these weather systems, and over many years the winds are fairly predictable. But because the systems are rarely stationary for long, winds are not as predictable as they are sometimes made out to be, and the direction and speed of frontal movements and pressure systems vary from place to place. In the northeastern United States, for example, the prevailing wind direction in autumn is from west to northwest. During any given autumn, however, the actual wind directions at the surface come from the prevailing direction only about half the time.

TRIGGERING MIGRATION
The earliest migration studies focused largely on the relationship between weather and the amount of migration: what weather condi-

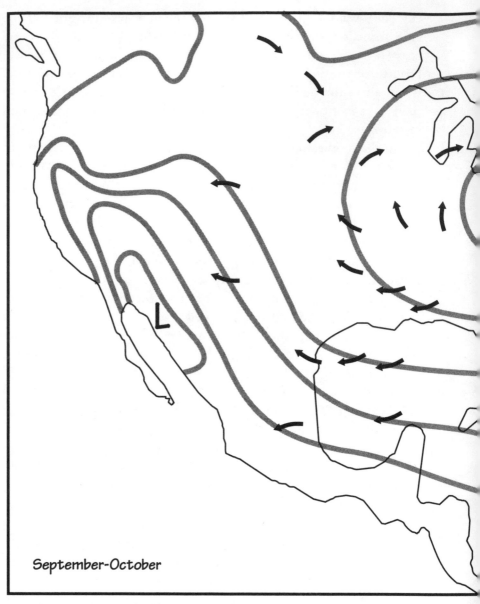

September-October

Winds (arrows) generally blow along isobars, areas of similar barometric pressure (gray lines); migrating birds go with the flow.

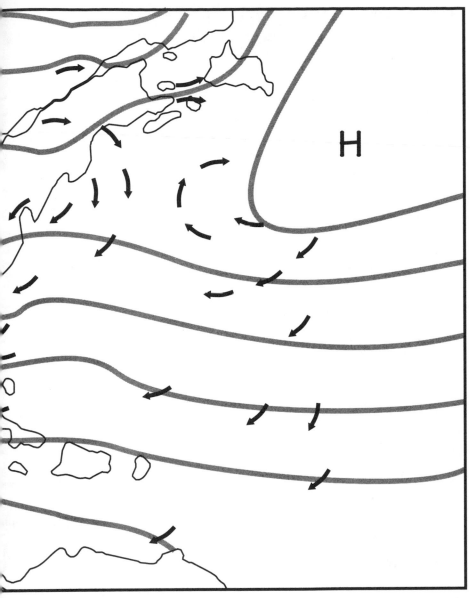

In autumn, high pressure over eastern North American creates westerly, clockwise winds that help migrants reach their wintering habitats.

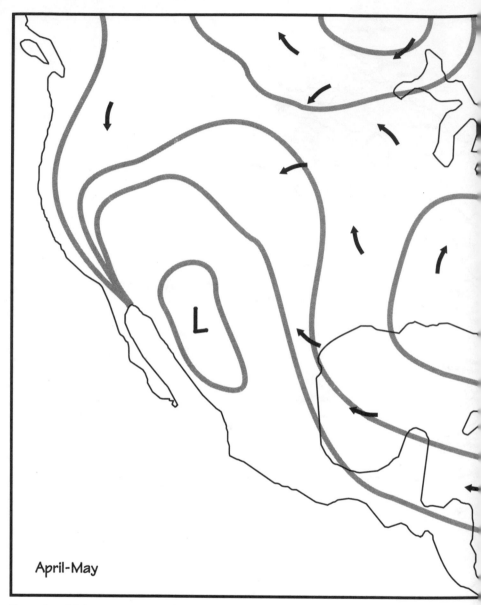

April-May

In spring, high pressure over the Atlantic pushes wind from the south across the Gulf of Mexico, helping birds fly northward.

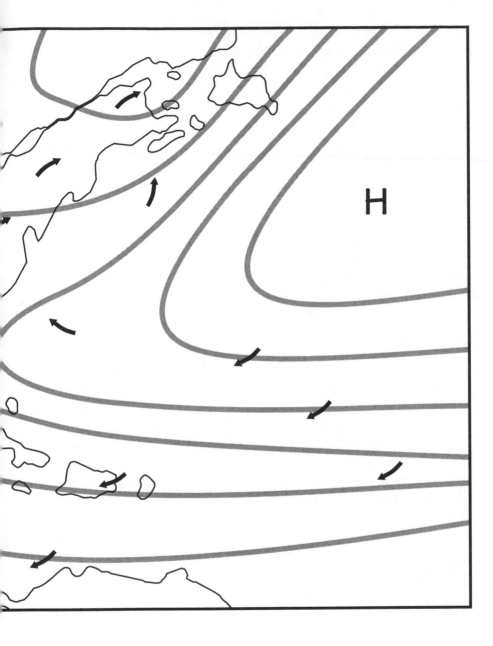

tions produced great numbers of migrants? Many of these researchers were birders, and by knowing what weather produced good flights of migrants, they could choose the best times for birding.

Studies of the association between bird migration and weather patterns have reinforced what many birders had known about migration for decades—that frontal movements are often correlated with large numbers of migrating birds. In autumn in much of the Northern Hemisphere, the migration of millions of birds is tied to the passage of cold fronts. These cold fronts act in two ways. First, they trigger migration in birds that have not yet started migration or among birds that are making migratory stopovers. This response may be due to the migrants' increased food requirements to meet the energy demands of lower temperatures. In cold weather birds require greater food intake to maintain body temperature. Just when they need more food, however, the cold causes some sources to disappear: insects die, water freezes, rodents hibernate, and so the birds must leave.

Second, cold fronts promote faster flight to winter habitats. Winds associated with cold fronts are usually favorable for migration, resulting in faster flight across the country. Fast flight has obvious advantages.

Closer to the tropics, where seasonal rains and monsoons dominate weather patterns, cold fronts are rare, so migration is not associated with fronts. Instead, tropical movements sometimes are timed to coincide with dry and wet seasons or with monsoons. Because the migration of tropical birds has been studied so infrequently, we actually know very little about it.

CASE STUDY	*Southbound Shorebirds Fly over the Western Atlantic with Cold Fronts.*

IN THE LATE 1960S W. JOHN RICHARDSON, THEN OF CORNELL UNIversity, witnessed the beginning of one of the most incredible migrations. Using radar, he observed the flight of thousands of shorebirds over the Nova Scotia coast. Flying southeastward, away from the shoreline, these birds were initiating a nonstop migration of more than 2,000 miles to the West Indies and South America. The radar revealed that intense shorebird movement occurred behind cold fronts with westerly winds. The birds were either close to the front or just behind it, and progressively fewer birds migrated in the days thereafter. Winds at flight time were usually from the west or northwest, so birds were assisted by tailwinds of 10 to more than 20 miles per hour. Ground speed of the flocks averaged about 45 miles per hour, so airspeeds were around 25 to 35 miles per hour. Although the species involved were not identified, it is likely that Golden Plovers, Hudsonian Godwits, and Semipalmated Sandpipers were among the migrants. A nonstop flight of 50 to 80 hours is required to complete this leg of their journey. ∎

CASE STUDY	*Southbound Songbirds Take Off with Cold Fronts.*

SONGBIRDS IN THE SOUTHEASTERN UNITED STATES INITIATE LONG flights over water with passing cold fronts. Ken Able, then of the University of Georgia, used radars in Athens, Georgia, and Lake Charles, Louisiana, to study songbird migrants in the late 1960s. He recorded "traffic rates" of songbirds as high as 50,000 to 200,000 birds per hour per mile of front. During five hours of nocturnal migration, up to a million songbirds passed through a one-mile-wide corridor. Able found that migrations were greatest with northerly winds, with falling temperatures, and after the passing of a cold front. At such times the radar was often saturated with migrants arriving on the northern coast of the Gulf of Mexico. Almost without exception, these songbirds were flying downwind to the south of west. More than sixty species of warblers, vireos, tanagers, orioles, flycatchers, gnatcatchers, sparrows, cuckoos, and others were migrating. ∎

| CASE STUDY | *Autumn Migrants in Southern Sweden Have Different Weather Preferences.* |

AT FALSTERBO, SWEDEN, TENS OF THOUSANDS OF BIRDS CAN BE SEEN during an autumn migration season—hawks, ducks, swifts, swallows, songbirds, gulls, and some others that migrate in daylight. Counts of these migrants permitted Tom Alerstam of the University of Lund, Sweden, to analyze the importance of various weather factors to individual species of migrants. Using counts of Common Buzzard, Common Eider, Wood Pigeon, Jackdaw, Yellow Wagtail, and Linnet, Alerstam found that favorable winds—in concert with absence of rain, increasing barometric pressure, dropping temperatures, and clear skies—produced the largest flights. Again, migration was associated with the passing of a cold front. There were differences among species, however: swifts select days with opposing or headwinds for migration, finches and starlings show only a slight preference for wind direction, Wood Pigeons and Jackdaws strongly select tailwinds, and buzzards select conditions favorable for soaring flight—those associated with an unstable boundary layer. ∎

Researchers have worked independently on different continents, with different types of birds, including both daytime and nocturnal migrants. They have also used a battery of complex statistical tests and sophisticated techniques to tease apart the relative importance of different weather variables like wind speed, wind direction, temperature, precipitation, and barometric pressure. They have asked whether wind direction is more important than temperature, whether wind is more important than barometric pressure, whether temperature is more important than the number of days since the passing of a cold front, and dozens of other questions. Their answers show that weather variables work not independently but together. That complicates the issue. Falling temperatures, for example, are usually associated with the passing of a cold front, a rising barometer, and westerly or northerly winds. To which of these aspects of weather do birds respond? It may be that they respond to a suite of variables.

Studies conducted in many places by many researchers have shown that certain frontal movements and other weather conditions consistently produce large numbers of migrants at a given location, and other conditions produce none. We birders have known some of this for a long time, of course: we know when to go where to find good birding.

ATMOSPHERIC STRUCTURE

Small-scale phenomena within larger weather systems influence the moment-to-moment flight of birds as well. These components of atmospheric structure include vertical and horizontal air movements and altitudinal differences in temperature, wind strength, wind direction, and humidity. Most important among these are the vertical and horizontal air movements within the atmosphere—turbulence, gradients, gusts, shears, and thermal updrafts.

What goes on in the air around us, mostly invisibly, is complex, and it is changing all the time. Nevertheless, there is a typical daily cycle to the atmosphere. Between the air that is literally around us and the free atmosphere high above is a transitional zone known as the boundary layer. The boundary layer is characterized by steep temperature gradients, strong wind gradients, and wind shears. This is where many migrants fly.

The depth of the boundary layer changes with time of day. Some atmospheric scientists call this the evolution, or development, of the boundary layer. Older texts, not taking into account its variability, report the atmospheric boundary layer as being about 1,500 feet deep. We now know that the boundary layer is shallower at night than during the day. Between sunset and dawn the boundary layer is stable, extending upward for only 600 to 900 feet. In early to midmorning, the boundary layer develops as the sun heats the earth and warm air begins to rise. Because the earth's surface is not uniform, some areas absorb heat more rapidly. At these locations air rises faster, forming columns of warm air within which vertical gusts can reach 10 miles an hour, or even more. These columns of warm, rising air—variously called thermal updrafts, thermals, or convective cells—are most abundant and strongest during late morning and midday, making this the best time for soaring migrants to be aloft. The top of the boundary layer usually marks the limit of thermals. In late afternoon, thermals lessen in strength, and they usually dissipate prior to sunset. It is dur-

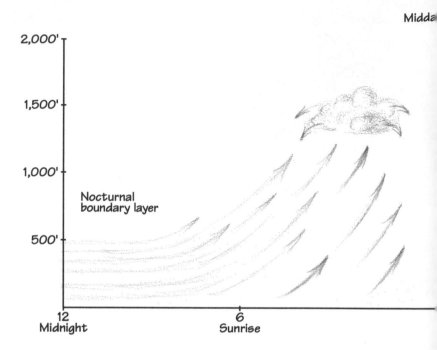

ing the last hour or so before sunset that the top of the boundary layer descends dramatically. Air between the thermals is less turbulent (more laminar and smooth) and wind is almost horizontal.

The location of thermals is difficult to predict, although their presence is sometimes betrayed by fluffy, fair-weather cumulus clouds, which often form at the top of thermals. If you examine these clouds carefully, you will see motion. Turrets, bubbles, columns, and other types of vertical substructure are often evident. The bottoms of these clouds are flat, marking the level in the atmosphere where condensation begins to form. Cumulus clouds can develop into cumulonimbus clouds with associated thunderstorms. Thermals that are not capped by cumulus clouds are referred to as blue thermals by some sailplane pilots; thermals can be extremely powerful, sometimes buffeting aircraft that fly through them.

One researcher has called thermals the ultimate structure of the atmosphere. Thunderstorms and tornadoes, for example, are similar in structure, only larger and more powerful. The shape of a thermal is roughly cylindrical, although Roland Stull, an atmospheric scien-

boundary layer

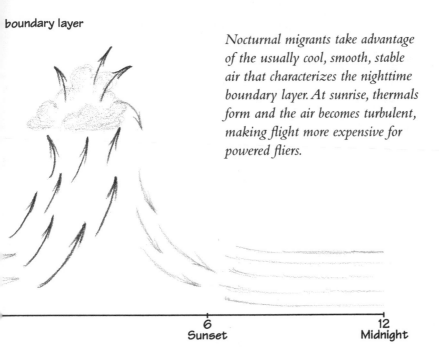

Nocturnal migrants take advantage of the usually cool, smooth, stable air that characterizes the nighttime boundary layer. At sunrise, thermals form and the air becomes turbulent, making flight more expensive for powered fliers.

6
Sunset

12
Midnight

tist at the University of Wisconsin, adheres to the "wurst" theory, likening the shape of a thermal to a sausage. Early hawk migration literature depicted thermals as doughnutlike vortices that floated with the wind. This is only partially correct, as this vortexlike shape occurs most often after thermals have become detached from the ground and when they are in their terminal stages.

A thermal layer may not form in very cloudy or rainy weather, and if it is rainy or foggy in the early morning, thermals will not form until the rain ends or the fog burns off. Another situation that inhibits thermals is called an inversion, which occurs when air temperature *increases* with altitude. In the normal daytime atmosphere, air gets colder at higher altitudes (up to a point). When high–altitude air is warm, thermals form but rise only to the inversion layer. Inversions at 1,000 to 2,000 feet are visible as hazy layers. Soaring flight is poor with these conditions.

In much of North America thermals do not rise higher than 5,000 to 6,000 feet on most days. In winter, thermals are less abundant and weaker than during other seasons. In spring and autumn,

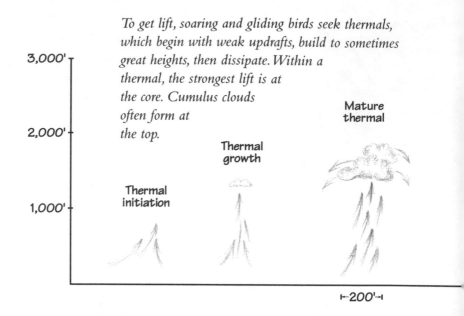

To get lift, soaring and gliding birds seek thermals, which begin with weak updrafts, build to sometimes great heights, then dissipate. Within a thermal, the strongest lift is at the core. Cumulus clouds often form at the top.

3,000'

2,000'

1,000'

Mature
thermal

Thermal
growth

Thermal
initiation

⊢200'⊣

during the peak migration seasons, thermals tend to be strongest. When thermals do not form, the depth of the daytime boundary layer will be similar to the nighttime layer, and the boundary layer will be stable.

In general the air at night is cooler and more laminar, with less turbulent air flow than during daytime, and this may be the reason so many birds migrate at night.

Thermals are only one form of turbulence. Wind is a most important atmospheric factor to migrants. Wind speed and direction change with altitude above the ground. Because of irregularities at the surface of the earth, friction impedes airflow and a gradient forms, with wind being slower closer to the surface. Although wind speed generally increases with altitude, the surface of the earth determines the rate of this increase: smooth surfaces like oceans and prairies experience stronger winds near the surface than areas where there are hills and forests. The wind gradient over the ocean is very steep within the first few feet above the surface. Over a forest, winds are impeded by irregularities, so winds just above the trees are slowed considerably and the gradient is not so steep as over prairie or water.

aximum thermal
development

Beginning of
dissipation

Thermal
dissipates

| CASE STUDY | *Migrating Hawks Rise and Fall with the Thermals.* |

SIDNEY GAUTHREAUX OF CLEMSON UNIVERSITY AND I USED MARINE radar to study the flight behavior of migrating Broad-winged Hawks during spring in south Texas. We monitored changes in altitude of migration starting from morning takeoff through midday. The rate of altitude change of migrants was about the same as the rate of thermal development—that is, the growth of thermals during the morning. The rate varied from day to day, from 200 to 300 feet per hour on poorer soaring days to 650 feet per hour on good soaring days. I conducted similar research in central New York with Ken Able and Vern Bingman of the State University of New York at Albany showed climb rates of about 450 feet per hour in midmorning— similar to the rate at which thermals rose. Some atmospheric scientists report "vertical growth rates" for the thermal layer of 400 to 1,100 feet per minute. ■

Wind direction also changes with altitude. In spring over the Gulf of Mexico, for example, daytime winds at 1,000 to 4,000 feet are often from the south, but at more than 5,000 feet they shift to the west.

CASE STUDY	*Songbirds Migrating over Switzerland Select Tailwinds.*

RESEARCHERS FROM THE UNIVERSITIES OF BASEL AND ZURICH, USING A tracking radar called the *Superfledermaus* to study the altitude, direction, and flight speed of songbirds migrating at night in the Swiss Alps, showed that birds are able to determine the direction and speed of the wind at different altitudes. They concluded that faster-flying ducks and shorebirds flew at higher altitudes than slower-flying songbirds. Most interesting was their finding that songbirds fly at altitudes with winds that promote a faster and more energy-efficient migration. They witnessed birds changing altitude to find the optimal altitude for migration. To do this, migrants must have the ability to gauge wind speed and direction and make decisions accordingly. ■

Birds are extremely sensitive to weather and atmospheric structure and select times and altitudes with the best wind directions and the best wind speeds. Frank Bellrose, a pioneer of American migration research at the University of Illinois, said it best: "Birds have a phenomenal understanding of winds."

The Travel Seasons

SUCCESS IN BIRDING IS BEING IN THE RIGHT PLACE AT THE RIGHT TIME. Birders know that migration "hot spots" offer the best birding—places where many individuals of many species are found when not breeding or wintering. Over the years, birders and scientists have learned when and where birds migrate, and we now have a wealth of information on the seasonal timing of migration. Appreciating the diversity and complexity of seasonal timing of migration helps us understand more how and why migration evolved and why there is so much variability in migration timing.

From a birder's perspective, the seasonal timing of migration describes the particular moment when a species migrates through a particular area. But from the birds' perspective, migration involves a long time and many places. The entire passage may take several weeks to more than three months. For a Swainson's Hawk that lives in Alberta, for example, autumn migration commences in mid-September and does not end until late October or even early November, some 6,000 kilometers (3,726 miles) to the south. How long it takes a migrant, what happens to the bird during its trip, how many days it must fly, and how many stopovers it must make—all of these aspects of migration are related to seasonal timing of migration.

The so-called autumn migration does not occur strictly in autumn, so a more accurate term would be postbreeding migration. "Spring migration" is not strictly correct, either; return migrations to a breeding site occur in mid- or late winter or in early summer in temperate and arctic climates, and so they should be called prebreeding migration. For example, Gyrfalcons migrate back to breeding cliffs in the Arctic in February, and Snowy Owls fly back to the tundra in February to March. This can hardly be called spring migration. Another example: some Sedge Wrens arrive at North American breeding sites in July, well past spring.

Among tropical birds, prebreeding movements are usually synchronous with the rainy season, and postbreeding migrations with the dry season, rather than with spring and autumn. Nevertheless, in this discussion I use the long-accepted terms autumn and spring migration.

THROUGH THE SEASONS AT CAPE MAY

The best way to illustrate differences in seasonal timing of migration among different birds is to describe a complete year of migration at one location. Seasonal timing of migration is better documented at Cape May than any other site in the Western Hemisphere. Located at 38 degrees north latitude, Cape May is far enough south and east that migrants from most of eastern North America can be observed there. Surprisingly, many southern and western species also pass through regularly. The tremendous variety of species that visit the area invites comparisons.

Autumn

Postbreeding migration in Cape May starts in late June with the arrival of the first southbound shorebirds. After breeding in the Arctic, such species as the Short-billed Dowitcher and Lesser Yellowlegs appear on mudflats of the Atlantic and Delaware Bayshore marshes, adults first. The males of some species migrate first, having fulfilled their reproductive obligation for the year and left the raising of the young to the females. More than a month later, young birds only 50 to 60 days old—called birds of the year—begin to arrive in Cape May after migrating more than 2,000 miles. By the end of September, much of the shorebird migration along the northeastern coast of the United States is completed.

A trickle of warblers is seen in Cape May in late July and early August, when a passing cold front brings Yellow Warblers, Prothonotary Warblers, Blue-winged Warblers, Louisiana Waterthrushes,

MIGRATION CALENDAR
FOR CAPE MAY, NEW JERSEY

January   Hawks.
Seabirds.
Waterfowl.

February   Seabirds.
Hawks.
Waterfowl.

March   Many waterfowl.
Seabirds.
Gulls.
Many hawks and non-Neotropical migrants.

April   Large numbers of non-Neotropical songbirds, water-
birds, and egrets and herons.
Gulls and terns.
First push of shorebirds and Neotropical songbirds.
Hawks continue strong.

May   Shorebirds.
Neotropical songbirds.
Some hawks.

June   Last of Neotropical songbirds and shorebirds.
First of southbound shorebirds.

July   Southbound shorebirds in full swing.
Neotropical songbirds.

August   Many shorebirds.
Neotropical songbirds.
First hawks head southward.

MIGRATION CALENDAR
FOR CAPE MAY, NEW JERSEY *(continued)*

September   Neotropical songbirds.
Non-Neotropical songbirds pick up.
Some shorebirds.
Hawks.
First big flights of cormorants, loons, and other
    waterbirds and waterfowl.

October   Last big push of Neotropical songbirds.
Gulls and terns.
Shorebirds wane.
Egrets and herons.
Owls.
Peak of hawks, cormorants, and scoters.
Many waterfowl.

November   Peak of waterbirds, gulls, and seabirds.
Non-Neotropical songbirds.
Peak of owls.
Hawks continue.

December   Late movements of non-Neotropical songbirds.
Last of hawks.
Seabirds and waterbirds.

American Redstarts, and Ovenbirds, in addition to Blue-gray Gnat-catchers, Bobolinks, and Orchard Orioles. A strong cold front that passed the night of August 8–9, 1989, brought thousands of individuals of more than ten species of warblers to Cape May. After the light migration in the first half of August, a cascade of migrants, mostly warblers, begins. By late August most songbirds that winter in the Neotropics are moving: tanagers, buntings, grosbeaks, orioles, vireos, thrushes, cuckoos, hummingbirds, and some others.

The main push of warblers is in the last week of August and the first weeks of September, by which time 15 to 30 species of warblers can be seen each day in Cape May. By the fourth week of September, most warblers have moved through, although Yellow-rumped and Palm warblers have just begun to migrate and will continue to pass through Cape May into December. Unlike the earlier migrating warblers, these species do not migrate to the Neotropics in large numbers.

Mid-September also marks the beginning of migration of songbirds that rarely move south of the United States, including kinglets, juncos, robins, towhees, and some sparrows, such as the White-throated Sparrow. The migration of these non-Neotropical songbirds continues into November and December.

Hawk migration in Cape May commences in mid-August with a few Ospreys, harriers, Bald Eagles, and kestrels. By the third week of September, large numbers of these, as well as Sharp-shinned Hawks, Merlins, Peregrine Falcons, and Cooper's Hawks are migrating. By October 10, most of these species have peaked, and the late-season hawks begin. During the last week of October and into the third week of November, Red-tailed Hawks, Red-shouldered Hawks, Golden Eagles, Bald Eagles, and Goshawks have reached their peak. By the last days of November, hawk migration is over, except for a few flights that follow cold fronts in December and even January.

Traditional wisdom knows little of these late-season hawk movements, though they consist of vultures, eagles, Red-tailed Hawks, Red-shouldered Hawks, Rough-legged Hawks, Sharp-shinned Hawks, and Northern Goshawks. Although the numbers are meager (perhaps a hundred a day), it is the types of birds that makes late-season hawk flights interesting.

Owls begin to migrate in late September, with Barn Owls first. Banding studies by the Cape May Bird Observatory show that adult Barn Owls precede immatures. By late October, hundreds and even thousands of Northern Saw-whet Owls are moving south, along with hundreds of Long-eared Owls. The peak season is the first third of November for these species, almost a month later than Barn Owls, and for these species immature birds precede adults by more than a week. The migration of Saw-whet and Long-eared owls continues into mid-December.

Along with hawks and songbirds, late-season migration includes waterfowl, loons, and seabirds. The last week of October through November marks the peak of the autumn migration for such species as Red-throated Loons, Northern Gannets, three species of scoters, Oldsquaws, Buffleheads, mergansers, and some others. During and after the late seabird and waterfowl migration come the alcids, kittiwakes, and more waterfowl that are shaken loose by cold weather in the northeastern United States and Canada. These movements occur throughout the winter.

Spring

In middle-latitude locations, such as Cape May, migration never seems to end. Birds pass through all year long, and sometimes it's hard to tell whether the migrants are coming or going. There are times of the year when southbound birds in postbreeding migration cross the flight paths of northbound birds in prebreeding migration.

Just as the autumn migration is ending in January, a few hardy birds start moving north to their breeding sites. Northern Harriers, Red-tailed Hawks, American Kestrels, Northern Gannets, and some waterfowl can be seen moving northward in February in fair weather. These movements often go unnoticed because the number of birds is small and few people are watching. The mid-March hawk counts at places like Sandy Hook, New Jersey, often record only a few adult male harriers and male kestrels, for example, because by this time, males of these species have commenced migration. In years with harsh weather, these males do not move through until late March and are therefore counted in greater numbers.

Late February and March also herald the northern movement of many species of waterbirds, including Red-throated Loons and Northern Gannets. American Woodcocks can arrive on breeding territories in Maine in March, despite snow and ice that make soil-dwelling prey inaccessible. Some woodcocks may even arrive in Cape May in February. These early migrants often die.

By March and April the migration in Cape May is in full swing. Waterfowl, finches, sea ducks, hawks, herons, egrets, sparrows, warblers, and many others are on the move. A few warblers and shorebirds are also about, and by late April new species are arriving daily. Thousands of Whimbrels are foraging and staging in the marshes behind the Atlantic coast barrier islands, where they eat fiddler crabs and other invertebrates. Slate-colored Juncos, Yellow-rumped Warblers, Palm Warblers, White-throated Sparrows, Pine Warblers, Yellow-throated Warblers, and Rufous-sided Towhees are among the songbirds that peak during this period.

During the last days of April warblers and other Neotropical migrants arrive in numbers and variety, but it is May that marks the peak of migration in Cape May for most songbirds and shorebirds returning from the Neotropics. The more than fifty species of songbirds include warblers, vireos, tanagers, orioles, flycatchers, catbirds, gnatcatchers, and thrushes. Each year New Jersey Audubon Society hosts the World Series of Birding on the second weekend in May because more species of birds are seen in New Jersey then than at any other time. During this premier birding event, more than forty teams from around the world move throughout New Jersey attempting to see as many species as possible in twenty-four hours. The winning team usually sees about two hundred species. The event raises more than $350,000 per year for conservation.

The last shorebird and warbler migrants pass through Cape May in early to mid-June. In the first week of June, tens of thousands of Semipalmated Sandpipers, Red Knots, Sanderlings, and Ruddy Turnstones are still feeding on horseshoe crab eggs along the Delaware Bay. By this time it may be too late for some of them to reach the tundra to breed; within a few weeks others will be winging it south, having left their mates on eggs or with young on the tundra.

THE CONTROL OF SEASONAL TIMING

The factors that are believed to control the onset of migration as well as the daily incidence of migration can be divided roughly into external, or exogenous, and internal, or endogenous, factors. The seasonal timing of migration can be controlled by both at different times or by one mediated by the other. Migration onset and seasonal timing are controlled genetically in some species and determined by weather, food, or social factors in others. Combinations of these factors are very difficult to study and even more difficult to separate.

Probably the most difficult aspect of seasonal timing of migration to study is genetic control. By breeding individuals from two different populations of a single species of migrant, researchers from the

Max Planck Institute in Germany showed that genetics is important in determining the seasonal timing of migration. They bred Black-caps, a warblerlike songbird, from southern Europe with Blackcaps from northern Europe. The behavior of the offspring was intermediate between the two parent populations. That is, the young showed migratory readiness, called *Zugenruhe,* that was later than the early-migrating northern population of Blackcaps yet earlier than the late-migrating southern population. This type of study is ingenious, and more crossbreeding experiments should be attempted.

CASE STUDY	*Northbound Long-Distance Songbirds Migrate Faster and Later in Spring.*

HOW DOES A MIGRANT THAT IS WINTERING IN VENEZUELA KNOW WHEN to return to its breeding site in Manitoba or Maine? Without any way to determine that the weather "back home" will be conducive for breeding, a long-distance migrant needs a mechanism that permits it to initiate spring migration at the correct time. John Hagan and his colleagues at Manomet Bird Observatory used banding data to examine differences in seasonal timing of migration between songbirds that fly long-distance to the Neotropics and those that do not leave North America. They found that in eastern Massachusetts the mean migration dates for long-distance migrants, such as Canada Warblers, American Redstarts, Red-eyed Vireos, and Swainson's Thrushes, were May 27 to 31. These dates were later than for such short-distance migrants as Ruby-crowned Kinglets, Hermit Thrushes, Yellow-rumped Warblers, and White-throated Sparrows. The sparrows, for example, passed through from April 29 to May 6, three weeks earlier than the Neotropical migrants. In addition, the variation in migration dates (both within and among years) was less in the Neotropical migrants than in the species that did not leave North America. Hagan and his colleagues concluded that the small variation in migration dates among migrants from the tropics, where day length is relatively constant, suggests that these birds have an internal, year-round clock that controls the onset of migration. The migrants that do not leave North America can rely on changing day length as a cue to migrate. ■

Weather

The seasonal timing of migration of some birds is more flexible (or plastic) than many people realize. The best examples of how weather has a direct control over migration can be seen in waterfowl and warblers. The long winter flights of Canada Geese and Yellow-rumped Warblers, although energy expensive, are cost effective. For the warblers the benefits of flying farther south in midwinter are better forage and milder temperatures. For the geese the advantage of returning early may be not just better forage but also getting an early start on the nesting season.

CASE STUDY	*Yellow-rumped Warblers in Arizona Flee Bad Weather.*

IN THE LATE 1970S RESEARCHERS NOTICED THAT YELLOW-RUMPED Warblers wintering in riparian forests in Arizona disappeared after periods of harsh weather. Within days, yellow-rumps became more abundant in habitats about a hundred miles to the south, in Mexico. It seems that these birds initiate migratory flights whenever weather is adverse and that these movements are not keyed to calendar date. Migratory behavior is probably controlled partly by an internal clock, and partly by external factors, such as weather and food. We still have not determined how the parts operate and how they interact. ■

CASE STUDY	*Canada Geese in Minnesota Fly a Reverse Migration.*

THE MIGRATION OF WATERFOWL IS CONTROLLED, IN PART, BY WEATHER. It is well known that some waterfowl disappear when lakes, ponds, and rivers freeze, then reappear when they thaw. Radiotelemetry studies of Canada Geese at a southern Minnesota wintering site reveal that in mild winter weather these birds will fly the entire 500 miles back to their breeding sites in southern Manitoba, where the lakes are still frozen, only to return a few days later. The movements of these birds are obvious on airport radars in the Twin Cities. Their flights resemble regular migration in all ways except that they are not done during what we normally consider the migration season. The movements back to the northern areas in winter are sometimes called reverse migrations because the birds appear to be traveling in the wrong direction. ■

CASE STUDY	*Carolina Juncos Migrate Up and Down.*

THE CAROLINA JUNCO, A SUBSPECIES OF JUNCO, BREEDS NEAR THE SUMmits of the Appalachian Mountains of the southeastern United States. Instead of migrating south in winter, as does the Dark-eyed Junco, it migrates down the mountains into adjacent valleys. The elevational migrations of Carolina Juncos have been studied for many years via color marking and tarsal bands. One of the most interesting findings is the return of male juncos to breeding territories during February. Because the flight is only ten or twenty miles up the mountains, these birds can visit their breeding sites with only a small expenditure of time and energy. If they encounter snow or harsh weather, they return to the valleys for several days or several weeks until conditions are more hospitable. Early arrival may afford some reproductive advantage—perhaps the earliest migrants get the best territories. ■

CASE STUDY	*Purple Martins Leapfrog from the Tropics.*

SPRING ARRIVALS OF PURPLE MARTINS IN NORTH AMERICA OCCUR AS early as late January and early February in southernmost Texas, Florida, and a narrow belt along the Gulf of Mexico. These birds settle into breeding territories as the next group leapfrogs over them to higher latitudes. By late March martins have reached Nebraska,

Purple Martins leapfrog up to North America in spring: the first birds to arrive stake out southern territories, and subsequent arrivals fly ever-farther northward.

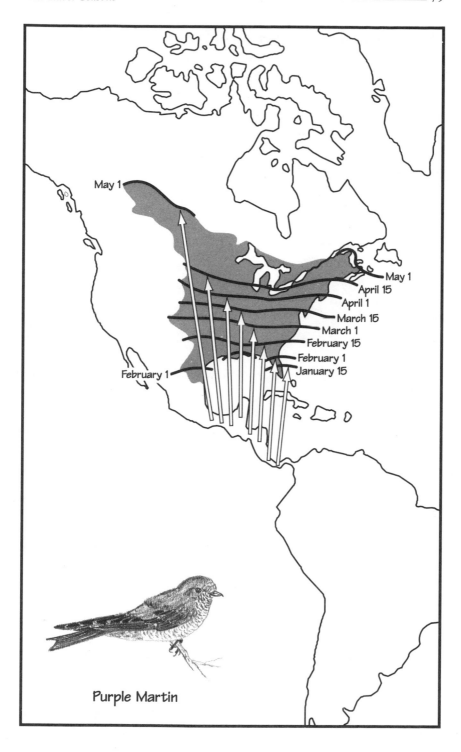

May 1
May 1
April 15
April 1
March 15
March 1
February 15
February 1
January 15
February 1

Purple Martin

Illinois, and the southern portions of Ohio, Pennsylvania, and New Jersey. The latest migrants do not arrive on territories in southern Alberta, Manitoba, southern Ontario, Quebec, and Nova Scotia until May. This wide range of arrival dates on nesting grounds shows how variable individuals and populations can be in their seasonal timing of migration. It also suggests that individuals from different geographic areas have different adaptive strategies. The cost of early migration can be dear. Being insectivores, martins face starvation in cold weather. I have seen martins die in southern Mississippi in early March, when the weather was cold and no insects were available. Similarly, martins that arrive in Cape May in late March or early April, when cold, wet days preclude foraging, become emaciated and listless and sometimes die. They are particularly susceptible to starvation because they have used their fat for migration. ∎

Prevailing Winds

Is migration timed to coincide with favorable winds? This is one of the most overlooked areas of migration research, but from the few studies that exist, it seems that birds do take advantage of seasonally predictable, favorable winds.

For example, the seasonal pattern of wind direction on the northern coast of Yucatan, where millions of songbirds initiate their trans-Gulf migration, is predictably from the south. During spring migration songbirds, shorebirds, and others leaving Yucatan and Central America can depend on tailwinds, which reduce both the energy and the time needed to return to North America.

In 1985 Sid Gauthreaux of Clemson University and I analyzed wind patterns in southernmost Texas to see how winds influence migrating raptors. We found that after February the winds became very predictable. On a majority of days from mid-March into May, the wind was from the south or south-southeast because of a relatively stationary high-pressure cell over Bermuda; it was responsible for the wind patterns over the Gulf and south Texas. Migrants of all kinds enjoyed a "free ride" during their return to North America in March through May.

Though it is difficult to say that wind has been an important evolutionary factor in shaping the seasonal timing of migration, it is likely that the spring departure dates of migrants from the Neotropics have been influenced not only by weather on the breeding grounds but also by wind conditions over the Gulf of Mexico. Birds that expect tailwinds over much of their journey back to North America can delay migration because they are guaranteed a speedy journey. If, on the other hand, headwinds were as likely as tailwinds, these birds would need several more days to migrate and thus have to leave the tropics earlier. It seems, then, that the initiation of spring migration has been shaped, at least in part, by prevailing seasonal wind patterns.

For many years it was believed that most, if not all, of the birds now known to be trans-Gulf migrants flew around the Gulf. The discovery that winds during spring migration are extremely favorable for the flight *across* the Gulf—much shorter in air miles than going around—means that the Gulf is less of a barrier to migrants than we once thought.

Wind patterns along the migration pathways of birds are not always favorable. Frank Moore and I compared the predictability of wind direction at two sites, one in Louisiana and one in New York. We found that wind direction in Louisiana was more predictable and favorable during spring than in autumn, and that spring winds in Louisiana were more predictable and favorable than either spring or autumn winds in New York. In New York, winds often have a westerly component—not usually helpful for northbound or southbound migrants.

This predictability of wind direction is of paramount importance. Because wind can be the greatest enemy of a migrating bird, an inappropriate response to wind can be fatal.

Throughout most of this chapter, I have examined the seasonal timing of migration for various species, each as a homogeneous unit. Remember, though, that individuals within a species may migrate at different times, depending on age, sex, or geographic population. Adults and immatures, males and females, and northern and southern populations of a species often fly different schedules or distances. Explanations for differences in the seasonal timing of migration lie in the social dominance of one class over another and the need for one class to arrive earlier than others on the breeding grounds.

| CASE · STUDY | *Male Warblers Precede Their Mates in Spring.* |

ONE OF THE FINEST STUDIES OF DIFFERENTIAL SEASONAL TIMING OF migration was done by researchers from Queens University working along the shore of Lake Ontario. From thousands of records collected over many years of banding, they learned that male warblers of more than twenty species returned to Canada several days earlier than females. The difference in timing between males and females ranged between one and four days. A similar study by Frank Moore, Ted Simons, and me showed that males migrated across the Gulf of Mexico to a barrier island off Mississippi earlier than females. The migrants in Mississippi were closer to the start of migration (Central and South America); those banded in Canada were near the end of their journeys, so the explanation was not that females migrate more slowly. Rather, we concluded, the males had left the tropics a few days before the females. If there is competition for nest sites or mates, it would be advantageous for males to hasten to the breeding grounds. ■

| CASE STUDY | *Female American Kestrels Migrate First in Autumn and Last in Spring.* |

FEMALE AMERICAN KESTRELS MIGRATE, ON AVERAGE, ABOUT THREE weeks to a month earlier than males during autumn in Cape May. During the last half of August and the first half of September, males are scarce, accounting for less than a quarter of the birds seen passing Cape May. A similar trend for this species was found at Hawk Mountain in Pennsylvania. Females may migrate early because they began molting while still brooding. Males presumably delay molt until the young have fledged because they must supply food to nestlings. Late-passing males and females at Sandy Hook, New Jersey, during spring are immature birds that have not yet bred—and may not breed that season. The reverse pattern holds in spring. At Sandy Hook, females don't become numerous until the end of March, when many males have already passed through. The majority of kestrel males found wintering at northern latitudes (New York and Pennsylvania) are males, most of them probably adults. Because this species relies on holes in trees and other cavities for nesting, choice nest sites are limited. If a male winters near his breeding site or arrives there early in spring, he can occupy a site before other males arrive. This could mean the difference between reproductive success and failure. ∎

THE ENIGMA OF EARLY MIGRATION

Although some species migrate to avoid the cold winter with its scarcity of food, many northern species migrate months before cold weather sets in. Among North American songbirds, early migration is a rule for such species as Louisiana Waterthrush, Blue-winged Warbler, American Redstart, Yellow Warbler, Prothonotary Warbler, Blue-gray Gnatcatcher, and Orchard Oriole. All commence migration in late July, months before insects and other resources disappear from their breeding habitats. Many of these species complete their migration to the tropics without ever facing temperatures cooler than 65 degrees Fahrenheit, and they certainly never experience autumn frost.

Some adult shorebirds, such as Short-billed Dowitchers, Lesser Yellowlegs, Semipalmated Sandpipers, and Least Sandpipers, are already southbound from the tundra in late June and early July. By late July and early August, the young of the year appear in temperate latitudes. These individuals have never seen autumn or winter or food scarcities.

Why do these birds leave the tundra so soon after—or even during—the breeding season when plenty of food is still available? Why do they begin a rigorous and dangerous southbound migration when there is no pressing need to fly south?

The early migration of songbirds and shorebirds suggests a southern ancestry of some species. That is, some of these species are more tropical in their heritage and visit the temperate, boreal, and arctic regions only long enough to breed. Their northbound migration and breeding activities are timed to take advantage of seasonally abundant food, usually insects.

A very different early migration occurs among some arctic species. The Snowy Owl, for example, migrates back to its tundra habitats earlier than practically any other species. During population ecology studies of Snowy Owls wintering in Alberta, Canada, Ross Lein and I found that adult females left their winter territories in late February and early March. Many had been winter residents on territories for three months. It seemed as though these birds had initiated "spring" migration, even though temperatures would be below freezing for another month or more. Yet these birds do not lay their first eggs until the last days of May or first days of June, three months after they initiate prebreeding migration. Why do adult Snowy Owls migrate so early? Perhaps it is because they must find abundant resources for breeding, and the whereabouts of these resources is unpredictable. Lemmings, on which the owls depend, are almost never abundant in the same place for two or three years in a row, so the owls must go wherever the lemmings are. An early exodus from the wintering area may allow adults a longer time to search for a site with enough food for successful reproduction. Immature owls remained in Alberta into late March and even early April. Because they do not breed in their first year, there is no need to risk early migration.

Gyrfalcons also migrate early. These birds lay their eggs two to three months earlier than Snowy Owls. The return of Gyrfalcons to nesting cliffs by late January or early February may reflect competition for a limited number of suitable sites, rather than competition for food. Unlike Snowy Owls, Gyrfalcons return to the same breeding grounds for many years, because their prey is more dependable than the lemmings on which Snowy Owls depend.

By Day or by Night?

AFTER DARK, MILLIONS UPON MILLIONS OF BIRDS FLY QUIETLY THROUGH the black skies above our heads. Although some birds move in daylight, they account for only a small proportion of all migrants; the vast majority of birds migrate at night.

Why are so many birds active at night? This fundamental question of daily activity cycles is related to the study of internal clocks, ecology, endocrinology, neurobiology, physiology, and evolution. Few researchers have studied the daily timing of migration, so we know little about when birds migrate during the 24-hour daily cycle or why birds fly at particular times. Even fewer have sought to answer the larger question, what evolutionary forces have shaped the daily timing of migration?

Although there is no easy way to separate nocturnal from diurnal, or daytime, migrants, some generalizations can be made. First, soaring birds almost always migrate during the day because they depend on thermal updrafts, available primarily in daytime, to provide lift. Second, birds that use powered flight are predominantly nocturnal migrants, although there are many exceptions. Some powered fliers do make daytime migrations, but these species tend to complete their migration within the colder latitudes or during late autumn and early spring, when daytime temperatures are cooler (we'll see why temperature is a factor later in this chapter). A majority of long-distance migrants, especially those that fly from temperate or arctic regions to the tropics, migrate at night.

SOARING MIGRANTS

Among soaring migrants, such as hawks, storks, pelicans, cranes, and swallows, the daily timing of migration is related to changes in the atmosphere. Because soaring migrants depend on thermals, migration cannot begin until the first thermals of the day form. This occurs earlier in the day in tropical and low latitudes than in higher latitudes. Birds can soar as early as 7:30 to 8:00 A.M. in tropical and subtropical areas, but soaring is not usually possible until an hour or two later in temperate latitudes. When thermals dissipate late in the afternoon, soaring migrants stop for the day. In most of the temperate zone birds can get in four to nine hours of soaring migration per day.

CASE STUDY	*Broad-winged Hawks in South Texas Await Thermals.*

WHILE STUDYING THE SPRING HAWK MIGRATION THROUGH THE RIO Grande Valley of southern Texas, I found that Broad-winged Hawks took off within three hours after sunrise. Early minutes of migration were marked by slow progress at low altitudes. Migrants emerged from the Santa Ana National Wildlife Refuge alone or with one or two other birds. They were joined quickly by others, forming small flocks as they moved north. On some mornings takeoff lasted forty-five minutes or longer and involved more than a thousand birds. Takeoff was earlier when skies were clear at dawn and later on days when clouds delayed the formation of thermals. On days with strong thermals, birds landed after 5 P.M., and on some days they stayed aloft until sunset, getting in seven to nine hours of migration. These birds flew at high altitudes before descending, so it seemed that thermals were strong until very late in the day. Such large-scale migration of soaring birds after 3 P.M. has not been reported from many sites. Migration at more northerly latitudes, for example, ends by 2 to 4 P.M. The bottom line: migratory hawks fly fewer hours in temperate areas than in tropical areas. ■

Migrating birds in the air

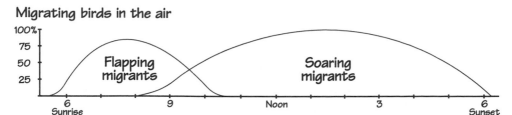

Flapping migrants fly primarily at night and in the early morning, when the air is calm and temperatures are cool. Soaring migrants fly during the day, when warmed air rises and gives them a literal lift.

Not all soaring migrants wait for thermals to commence. By using power-assisted glides when updrafts are not strong, such species as Sharp-shinned Hawks can take off earlier than birds that must soar, like Broad-winged Hawks. At Hawk Mountain Sanctuary in Pennsylvania, Sharp-shinned Hawks and some other migrating raptors begin migrating near dawn because lift along the ridges is abundant. Away from the ridges they also sometimes take off before thermals form but must then incorporate flapping flight to provide some of the needed lift. The energy needed to migrate is, consequently, greater than for birds that only soar. These early flights are almost always at lower altitudes than thermal soaring later in the day.

POWERED MIGRANTS

Takeoff time is known for many nocturnal migrants. Researchers have determined this in many places and seasons using radar, ceil-

Nocturnal migrants in the air

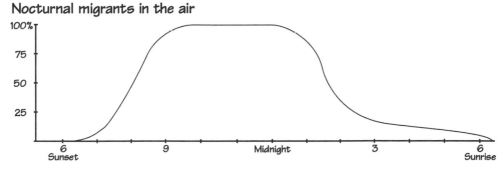

The peak of nighttime migration occurs from an hour after sunset until after midnight; most birds land by sunrise.

ometer, and direct observation. The results of study after study show that migration is initiated thirty minutes to an hour after sunset. Among the North American songbird species in this group are the warblers, tanagers, vireos, orioles, kinglets, thrushes, gnatcatchers, many sparrows, cuckoos, catbirds, and thrashers. The same is true for shorebirds, owls, herons and egrets, and waterfowl.

The cessation of nightly migration varies more than takeoff timing. Radar and ceilometer tell us that the peak of migratory activity occurs mostly between two and four hours after sunset and that the number of birds diminishes greatly after four to six hours after sunset. In temperate North America, this means the peak of migration occurs before 10 P.M. to midnight, after which the number of migrants aloft tapers. On many nights there are few or no birds in the air in the hours before dawn.

CASE STUDY	*Owl Migration at Cape May Point Begins Just after Sunset.*

USING A NIGHT-VISION SCOPE AT CAPE MAY POINT, RESEARCHERS found that the largest numbers of owls were seen in the first two to three hours after sunset. The owls were predominantly saw-whets, with smaller numbers of Barn and Long-eared owls. Banders, however, were able to capture more owls in the four hours before sunrise. The high capture rate before dawn was presumably a result of owls' selecting hunting or resting sites after migration had ended— the birds captured before dawn were not actively migrating. Like songbird migration, then, owl migration apparently begins just after sunset and continues for a varying portion of the night. ∎

CASE STUDY	*Northbound Songbirds along the Gulf Coast Take Off Just after Sunset.*

EACH SPRING MILLIONS OF MIGRATING WARBLERS, TANAGERS, ORIOLES, vireos, thrushes, and other songbird migrants arrive on the northern coast of the Gulf of Mexico following a nonstop flight from the

Yucatan region of Central America. After landing during daylight hours, these birds feed and rest in the woods until sunset, when most resume their migration. In the late 1960s James Hebrard, a graduate student from Louisiana State University, observed the takeoff of these birds using a ceilometer aimed horizontally above the treetops. He found that nearly all birds took off within an hour and a half after sunset, with the average being forty-five minutes. On a nearby radar takeoff looked like an explosion with a long tail, corroborating the graduate student's findings. This simultaneous use of ceilometer and radar was unique. ∎

CASE STUDY	*Shorebirds Await High Tide on the Coast, but Sunset at Inland Sites.*

SEMIPALMATED SANDPIPERS ARE SMALL SHOREBIRDS THAT WEIGH between 20 and 30 grams—about an ounce. They make long-distance migrations between the North American tundra and South America. A comparison of a coastal, tidally inundated site with an inland, nontidal site revealed that migratory flights began earlier (sometimes a few hours before sunset) at the coastal site when the tide was high in late afternoon and evening. Because birds at the tidal site could not forage at high tide, they began migration earlier. At the inland site, migration always began after sunset. Comparing takeoff time at those two sites confirms that takeoff is a plastic behavior subject to environmental input.

Radar studies in coastal Nova Scotia also showed takeoffs of shorebirds before sunset when tides were high. These birds were also initiating long-distance migration, sometimes to South America via routes over the western Atlantic. Out of necessity, much of this flight occurs during daylight hours. Although these results apply to a limited number of species, they have implications for the evolution of nocturnal migration. They show that this behavior is controlled in part by genetics and in part by the environment. ∎

Although many more birds migrate at night than during the day, some species are true daytime migrants: blackbirds (Red-winged

Blackbirds, Brown-headed Cowbirds, and Common Grackles), finches, crows, and Blue Jays. Most migrate shorter distances than nocturnal migrants.

Many species considered daytime migrants are actually crepuscular: they do much of their migration flight just before and just after sunrise. A radar study in England showed that many daytime migrants, finches among them, begin migration about two hours before sunrise and land within three hours after.

For night migrants the trigger for daily timing of migration seems to be the setting sun; for daytime migrants, the rising sun. In the 1950s, German biologist Gustav Kramer discovered that some caged migratory birds displayed a curious behavior. After the sun set, they hopped almost incessantly, sometimes for several hours. This behavior he termed *Zugenruhe,* which means nocturnal restlessness. By manipulating the lights in a laboratory, Kramer was able to re-schedule sunset for the birds. When "sunset" was delayed for an hour or two, *Zugenruhe* occurred an equal amount of time later. When "sunset" was moved ahead, so was the birds' response. Thus, the setting of the sun seems to set the internal clocks of some migrants.

Cages and artificial light to test nocturnal restlessness have become standard in the research programs of many migration scientists. Even more important, nocturnal activity has been used to study the circadian (day) and circannual (yearly) clocks of birds and the neuroendocrine connection between those biological clocks and bird behavior.

THE ADVANTAGES OF NIGHT FLIGHT

Explaining how and why nocturnal migration evolved is, for me, the most challenging question about daily timing of migration. Several explanations have been proposed, but no single hypothesis explains the daily timing of migration of all birds. One of the earliest explanations for nocturnal migration focused on the need to avoid predators. Smaller birds, such as warblers and vireos, reduce their chances of being preyed upon by flying at night, but not significantly. Brant geese, ducks, egrets, and other large birds are also nocturnal migrants, but predator avoidance is not a likely reason. Another explanation that does not survive close scrutiny is the hypothesis that the night sky offers better cues for orienting and navigating. Although stars are out at night, the sun, polarized light, magnetism, and other cues now thought to be used in avian orientation are available during daytime.

There are two more plausible explanations of nocturnal migration. The first, called the daytime foraging hypothesis, is that birds need to forage in daylight before undertaking long, arduous flights. Although this is logical, some waterfowl, shorebirds, and owls forage at night, and yet they are also nocturnal migrants.

Perhaps the best explanation of nocturnal migration focuses on the physiology and aerodynamics of avian flight. After all, flight is the single most important characteristic that distinguishes birds from other vertebrates. Recently, Frank Moore of the University of Southern Mississippi and I proposed that atmospheric structure is the strongest selective force shaping the daily timing of migration. We further proposed that other selective pressures, including the need to forage in daylight, may work in concert with atmospheric structure to influence this fundamental aspect of migratory flight behavior.

Our atmospheric structure hypothesis states that the predictable daily sequence of changes in atmospheric structure have shaped the behavior of migrants so that it is advantageous for powered migrants to fly at night and for soaring migrants to fly at midday. The nocturnal atmosphere is more conducive to powered flight, especially long-distance flight, because it is cooler and more laminar (smoother) than during daytime. Cooler air at night is important because powered migrants generate an enormous amount of heat. Starlings and other birds with resting body temperatures of 100 to 102 degrees Fahrenheit (38 to 39 degrees Celsius) elevate their temperatures to 105 to 111 degrees Fahrenheit (41 to 44 degrees Celsius) during powered flight. Cloacal temperatures of Sharp-shinned Hawks caught during active migration in Cape May sometimes exceeded 108 degrees Fahrenheit (42 degrees Celsius), a lethal temperature for human beings.

Body temperature can be reduced by two mechanisms during flight. Convective cooling, a result of air moving across the skin, is substantial. A second means of cooling is evaporative loss of water during respiration and through the skin. When migrants metabolize the fat they use for fuel, water is produced that can be used for thermoregulating. During long, nonstop flights such as those over water or a desert, body water may be more limiting than fat. Evaporative water loss increases with air temperature: more water is lost at higher temperatures than at low temperatures. Cool night air, however, promotes convective heat loss, thereby reducing evaporative water loss. During spring and autumn in the United States daytime air temperatures often exceed 70 to 90 degrees Fahrenheit (21 to 32 degrees Celsius) and average some 9 to 14 degrees Fahrenheit (5 to 8 degrees Celsius) higher than at night.

The second advantage of nocturnal migration is that birds can maintain a straight, level course through the more stable and more laminar night air. This is especially important for small birds that fly at relatively slow airspeeds. Most migrants fly 15 to 45 miles per hour (8 to 20 meters per second) and are buffeted by normal updrafts of 2 to 6 miles per hour that occur in midday when thermals are abundant. Between 10 A.M. and 3 P.M. convective turbulence reaches a maximum. Maintaining straight, level flight in turbulent air is energy expensive because a bird must constantly correct for updrafts and gusts. Turbulence may also make it difficult for a bird to orient itself.

The daily timing of migration is related to the seasonal timing of migration, which is itself related to atmospheric structure. The postbreeding, southbound migration of many arctic shorebirds and temperate songbirds that migrate to the tropics begins in early to midsummer; shorebirds along the Atlantic coast begin in late June, and warblers begin in late July. By the first week of September the migration of most songbirds and shorebirds that fly to the Neotropics is well under way. From July into September, midday convective turbulence (both thermal columns and random movements) is stronger, which makes flight difficult. Moreover, air temperatures exceed 70 degrees Fahrenheit or even 90 degrees Fahrenheit (20 to 30 degrees Celsius). In that heat, birds have difficulty regulating their body temperature and must resort to evaporative cooling, with its accompanying loss of water. The logical alternative is to migrate at night.

The diurnal migratory flights of some songbirds might seem to refute the atmospheric structure hypothesis, but when examined closely, this exception actually proves the rule. Many of the songbirds that are classified as diurnal migrants initiate flights one or two hours before sunrise and terminate their flights within three to five hours after. They are crepuscular rather than truly diurnal. And the period around sunrise is characterized by low air temperatures and minimal thermal turbulence. These birds avoid flying at midday, when the air is warm and the atmosphere is least conducive to powered flight. Most waterfowl, loons, and other species also migrate early and late in the day, probably for the same reasons.

Another example of diurnal flight that seems to contradict the atmospheric structure hypothesis is the morning flight of songbirds that are normally nocturnal migrants. Professor Sidney A. Gauthreaux of Clemson University has proposed that these movements are redirected migration following wind drift during the previous night's migration. Other researchers have argued that morning flight is simply a continuation of the previous night's flight. At Cape May Point, New Jersey, where several birders and I studied morning flight during the postbreeding, southbound migration, migrants flew *north* after dawn. They might have been correcting for drift but were more likely seeking habitat for a migratory stopover. These birds commence their flights at or before dawn and end them within one to three hours of sunrise. Both the "diurnal" songbird migrants and those making morning flights fly before the atmosphere becomes warm and turbulent.

THE EVOLUTION OF NOCTURNAL MIGRATION

There are at least two scenarios by which nocturnal migration could have evolved. Both assume that the earliest migrants were diurnal migrants that traveled only short distances at first but then found reason to fly farther—more food or better nesting sites. As these diurnal flights became longer, according to the first hypothesis, energy needs became greater and benefits accrued to individuals who flew in the evening or early morning. Gradually migratory flight became more nocturnal. It is possible that some of the crepuscular migrants—the birds active during the transitional period between night and day—are in the process of becoming nocturnal migrants. This theory assumes a gradual change of behavior from shorter- to longer-distance migration.

The second scenario relies on migration across lakes, seas, deserts, mountain ranges, or other barriers that require long, nonstop flight. In this hypothesis, selective pressure acted rapidly. The amount of energy required increased dramatically with long, nonstop flights, as did the danger associated with migration. Risks are far greater for long-distance crossings of barriers than for short flights over less hostile habitat. And migrants that make long, nonstop flights lose substantial quantities of water through evaporative cooling, even though the conversion of fat to energy has some water as a by-product. The Gulf of Mexico, the Mediterranean Sea, the Sahara Desert, portions of the western Atlantic Ocean: many of these barriers are located in tropical, subtropical, or at least warm climates, whose high daytime temperatures are not conducive to long flights. So avoiding hyperthermia became a necessity, and birds began migrating at night.

Whether it happened gradually or rapidly, one clue to the evolution of the daily timing of migration lies in the distance a species migrates. The migrants that are most nocturnal are the songbirds and shorebirds that fly long distances from higher latitudes to the tropics. Those shorebirds and songbirds that make shorter trips and do not leave temperate latitudes are more likely to migrate during daytime. Raptors and other soaring birds migrate almost entirely by day, commencing their flights several hours after sunrise and ending several hours before sunset. Because soaring migrants depend on the updrafts produced by thermal turbulence, natural selection has forced hawks, pelicans, and other soaring birds to migrate in midday.

Because nocturnal migration is so widespread among avian migrants, it is likely that it has evolved independently in many groups of birds. It is also likely that the selective force that caused the evolution of nocturnal migration is very strong and acts on most species that migrate. The available evidence suggests that the atmosphere is a potent selective force in the evolution of daily timing of migration. Adaptations that reduce the costs and risks of migration, such as judicious timing, will be favored by natural selection. The advantage of migrating at night is flight in cool, smooth air that promotes convective cooling and a faster and more energy-efficient flight. Other selective forces cannot be discounted, however, and it is likely that the need to feed during daylight has also been an important factor in the evolution of nocturnal migration.

SEVEN

Barriers to Migration

THE AIRPLANE KNOWS NO BARRIERS TO TRAVEL. BUT IN PAST CENTURIES, long-distance crossings of oceans, deserts, and mountain ranges required careful preparation. Similarly, migratory birds are confronted by barriers. Look at a topographic map of the world: there are few places where birds will not encounter obstacles—a large body of water, a mountain range, a prairie, a desert, a forest, or some other geographic feature—that impede migration. The ways birds deal with such barriers are as diverse as most other aspects of migratory flight. Some species cross large bodies of water without hesitation; others never fly over large lakes. Each species has adaptations that help it deal with barriers.

Most birds cannot swim for long distances, so they must either cross large bodies of water without stopping or fly around. A desert is a similar barrier. Although a songbird can survive a short stay at an oasis or even in bushes or among rocks, a desert stopover could be disastrous for species accustomed to forest, marsh, or swamp. Similarly, forests are poor stopover sites for such species as sandpipers, rails, ducks, and loons. Picture a loon or a scoter landing in a forest, corn-field, or pasture—or a songbird landing on the ocean. Either scenario would mean death: loons cannot take off from land, and larks cannot swim. Waterbirds that make overland crossings often do so in long hops, flying from one large body of water to another; similarly, land birds often fly over water in long hops, using islands as resting sites.

Because they are barriers to many migratory species, bodies of water and their adjacent land masses have shaped migratory pathways. In North America the Gulf of Mexico, the Atlantic and the Pacific oceans, and the Great Lakes have been the most prominent selective forces in determining migratory pathways and behavior. Millions of birds collect along the coastlines of these bodies of water, resting and foraging until ready to resume their migration. New Jersey, located between the Delaware Bay and the Atlantic Ocean, is like a giant funnel; birds avoiding these waters eventually find their way to Cape May. Because of the enormous numbers of birds that land there during migration, coastal areas are some of the most important stop-over sites.

SOARING BIRDS AND WATER BARRIERS
Soaring birds frequently fly around, rather than over, a body of water because the thermal updrafts on which they depend for energy-efficient travel are weak and widely dispersed over water. Soaring flight over water is therefore difficult and dangerous. For these birds, passage over water would require powered flight, for which some species do not have enough energy. And in fact, raptors sometimes drown while attempting to cross Lakes Superior, Michigan, and Erie.

To avoid strenuous and dangerous water crossings, most hawks, pelicans, and other soaring migrants fly around the western end of the Gulf of Mexico. That is why the autumn and spring migrations through south and east Texas provide such good opportunities for birders. Hawk watchers know that the Rio Grande Valley and sites near Corpus Christi and Galveston are excellent places to look for migrating Broad-winged Hawks. During autumn, more than a hundred thousand of these birds have been seen in a single day in Texas and Louisiana. These migrants can form continuous streams, sometimes passing observers at the rate of more than 10,000 birds per

Southbound birds reluctant to fly over the Atlantic follow the coastline and are funneled into Cape May, where they confront the Delaware Bay. Large concentrations of many species wait here for calm weather before making the crossing.

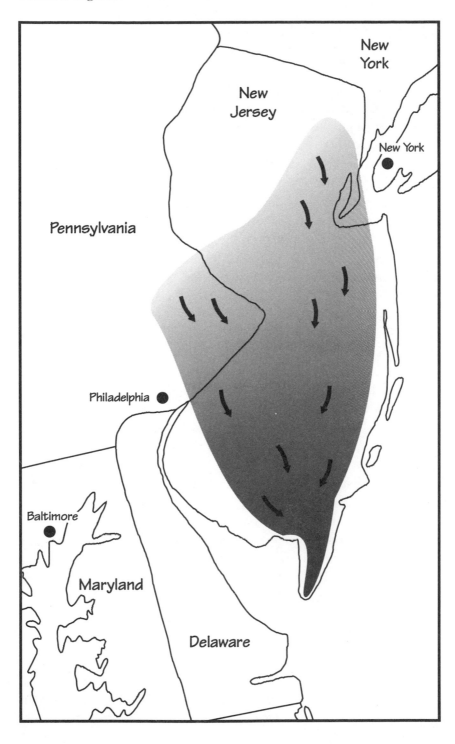

hour. The exact locations of the major flights or flight lines from year to year are not predictable in these areas, although hawk watchers continue to search for them.

In several places in Europe water barriers act as funnels, aggregating tens of thousands of soaring migrants. The Mediterranean Sea is the most prominent of these; migrating soaring birds congregate at opposite ends of the sea. The Straits of Gibraltar at the western end and Bosporus at the eastern end offer excellent opportunities to see thousands of migrating raptors, storks, pelicans, and cranes. A third, and lesser, pathway goes through Italy and then island-hops across the Mediterranean to Tunisia or Libya via Sicily and Malta.

Falsterbo, at the southernmost tip of Sweden, hosts a migration of thousands of hawks and cranes, along with many more thousands of songbirds, swallows, and other migrants. During autumn this funnel for the Scandinavian peninsula is the European equivalent of Cape May.

In Southeast Asia hundreds of thousands of land birds are funneled into the southern portion of the Malayan peninsula, where they encounter the Strait of Malacca. At the southernmost part of the peninsula, hundreds of thousands of land birds, including many soaring species, cross about 13 miles (18 kilometers) of water to reach the Sumatran islands. This crossing is not well known, but the concentration of Asian migrants offers one of the most exotic birding experiences on the globe.

The most spectacular aggregation of soaring birds in the world occurs in Israel, the land bridge between Eurasia and Africa, with the Indian Ocean and the Red Sea on one side and the Mediterranean on the other. At least two million soaring migrants pass through Israel each autumn to avoid water crossings. After wintering in Africa, the survivors return via the same land bridge, where they are most visible in Eilat.

Soaring birds, for whom flapping flight is too costly, avoid crossing water. Broad-winged Hawks go south through the Central American land bridge, and return via the same route.

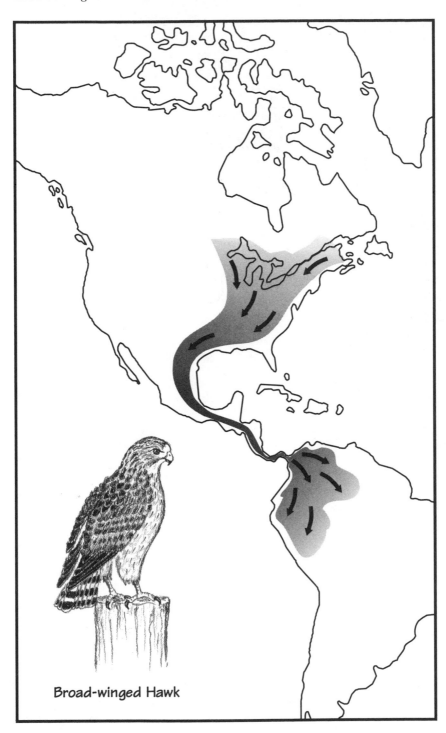

Broad-winged Hawk

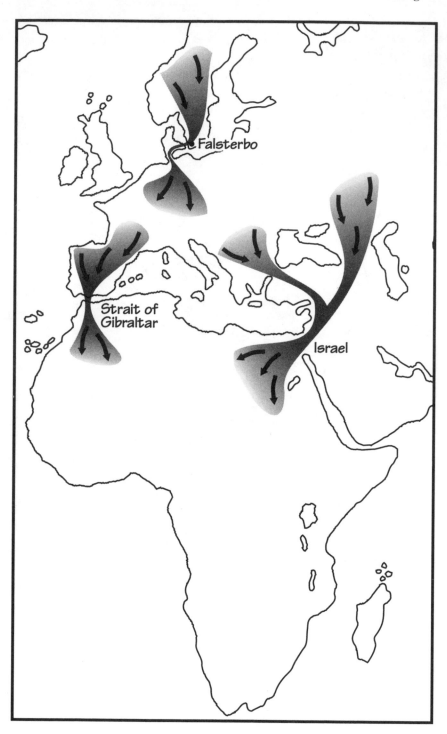

| CASE STUDY | *Raptors Migrate around the Mediterranean.* |

SINCE THE EARLY 1980S, THE SOCIETY FOR THE PROTECTION OF NATURE in Israel has counted migrating hawks and other soaring birds as they fly through Israel. Beginning in August, nearly two million hawks, eagles, kites, falcons, vultures, and other raptors funnel through Israel on their migration from eastern Europe and Asia to Africa. In spring counters at Eilat may see more than a half million hawks of twenty-odd species. Flocks of Lesser Spotted Eagles and Honey Buzzards have numbered forty thousand to seventy thousand. Radar has been used to determine the geographic distribution of these migrants. Standardized counts of hawks passing through Israel will enable researchers to monitor the stability of populations that breed in Europe and Asia. The interest in raptor numbers and their pathways through Israel is related to air traffic. Imagine flying a fighter jet at 500 miles (800 kilometers) per hour through a flock of a thousand eagles, hawks, pelicans, storks, or cranes. A fighter jet's bulletproof windscreen is no match for a hawk. The Israeli Air Force has lost many pilots and planes to collisions with birds and therefore monitors the birds' movements. The same hazards exist in the United States. In fact, the U.S. Air Force has a special committee called Bird Air Strike Hazard (BASH) to deal with the problem. ∎

A few raptor species do make long-distance water crossings. The longest crossings are made by the small Amur Falcon, which flies more than a thousand miles over the Indian Ocean between India and eastern Africa. Documentation for this behavior is anecdotal. According to one source, these birds fly from northeastern China to the west coast of India, where they forage until fat (which makes them a prized delicacy among the locals). The water-crossing behavior of Amur Falcons would make an excellent study.

Migration corridors follow land bridges and short water crossings. Millions of hawks and other birds fly over the Strait of Gibraltar or through Israel. Falsterbo, in southern Sweden, is a funnel much like Cape May.

Common Buzzard

CASE STUDY	*Honey Buzzards Go Island-Hopping.*

SPRING MIGRATION COUNTS OF THOUSANDS OF HONEY BUZZARDS (A medium-sized, insectivorous hawk) along the shore of Calabria in southern Italy show that these birds do make short-distance water crossings. These hawks were crossing the Straits of Messina from Sicily during their return to European breeding sites, part of an island-hopping migration involving flights of more than 100 miles (160 kilometers) over water. The first leg of the journey is from Tunisia and Libya to Malta (more than 200 miles or 320 kilometers), the second is from Malta to Sicily (more than 60 miles or 96 kilometers), and the third is from Sicily to the European mainland (about 12 miles). Other hawks involved were the Hobby, Black Kite, Osprey, Peregrine Falcon, Hen Harrier, and European Kestrel. ∎

CASE STUDY	*Hawks Cross Water When the Wind Is Right.*

TO LEARN HOW ANIMALS MAKE DECISIONS, I STUDIED THE BEHAVIOR OF migrating hawks at Cape May Point and at the end of Whitefish Peninsula in Michigan's Upper Peninsula. Hawks migrating southward at Cape May encounter a 13-mile (18-kilometer) crossing where the Delaware Bay empties into the Atlantic Ocean. As a bird looks toward Delaware, it has the vastness of the Atlantic to its left and a similar view to its right. At Whitefish the crossing is about 18 miles (29 kilometers), but islands and land are visible on the opposite side. Peregrine Falcons, Merlins, Ospreys, and Northern Harriers, which have long, almost pointed wings and are capable of strong powered flight, showed little or no reluctance to cross at Whitefish or Cape May and crossed in almost any weather. Broad-winged Hawks, Turkey Vultures, and Red-tailed Hawks, on the other

Southbound Common Buzzards choose the short crossing at the Strait of Gibraltar or the overland route through the Bosporus and Israel.

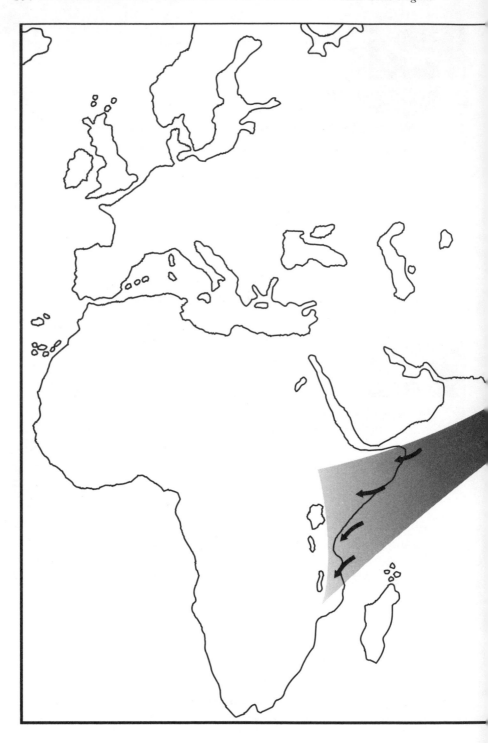

*One of the longest water crossings undertaken by a raptor is the
route of the Amur Falcon across the Indian Ocean. This bird breeds
in northeastern China and winters in Africa.*

Amur Falcon

hand, rarely crossed; these species cannot undertake long powered flights. The smaller Sharp-shinned Hawks and American Kestrels were most interesting to watch because they made decisions to cross or not to cross based on weather. When winds were strong, most birds were reluctant to cross. They descended to low altitudes, turned at the end of the peninsula, and went back inland. Some birds began crossings, apparently sampling the flight conditions, and returned to shore. With light winds, Sharp-shinned Hawks and American Kestrels approached the tips of these peninsulas at very high altitudes and crossed in good numbers. The changes of behavior with atmospheric conditions demonstrated that the birds made decisions. ∎

WATER CROSSINGS BY POWERED MIGRANTS

Unlike soaring migrants, powered migrants do not depend on updrafts to help them cross bodies of water, but they must generate all the necessary energy themselves. For long-distance crossings, the amount of energy needed is formidable.

Many of the same bodies of water that influence soaring birds also shape the migration behavior and ecology of powered migrants. The major oceans, gulfs, seas, and large lakes all are barriers that require special adaptations. In some cases birds cross them; in others they fly all or most of the way around.

Crossings of the Gulf of Mexico are probably the best understood of long-distance water crossings. Birds that traverse the more than 600 miles (1,000 kilometers) of the Gulf range in size from somewhat more than a pound (500 grams) to slightly less than ⅕ ounce (5 grams). Imagine that birds weighing less than an ounce undertake such a demanding journey: for the price of one airmail stamp, you could mail two Black-and-White Warblers or five Ruby-throated Hummingbirds from anywhere in the United States to Mexico—although most migrants arrive in better shape when they fly there themselves.

Prothonotary Warblers use favorable winds to help
them cross the Gulf of Mexico during
both spring and fall.

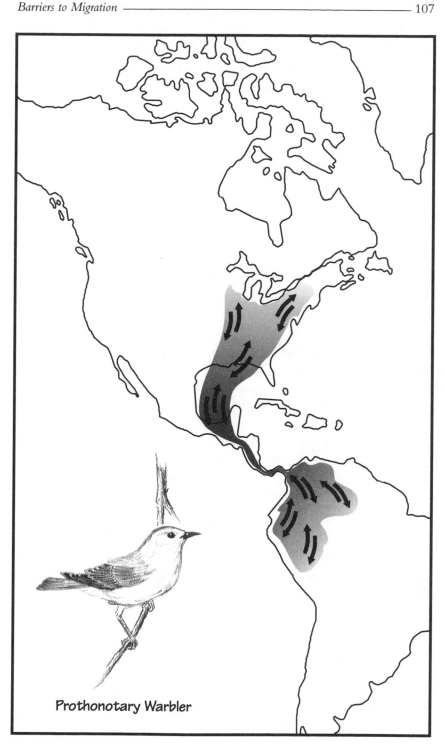

Prothonotary Warbler

A Hooded Warbler weighing about ⅓ ounce (10 grams) can fly for more than 600 miles nonstop across the Gulf of Mexico. More than fifty other songbird species (at least six vireos, thirty-six warblers, eleven flycatchers, two tanagers, two orioles, one catbird, one bobolink, one Dickcissel, one grosbeak, two cuckoos, one sparrow, four thrushes, two buntings, one gnatcatcher, and one humming-bird)—totaling millions of individuals—cross some portion of the Gulf of Mexico in both spring and autumn. Blue-winged Teal, Cattle Egrets, and some larger birds also fly over the Gulf. These birds initiate flights from as far south as Honduras just after sunset and fly nonstop for up to twenty-four hours before reaching the U.S. coastline between Texas and Florida. With prevailing south winds, the flight takes about fifteen hours, so birds often make a landfall in late morning.

CASE STUDY	*Shorebirds and Blackpoll Warblers Cross 2,000 Miles of Ocean.*

ONE OF THE ENDURANCE FLIGHT RECORDS FOR BIRDS IS THE NONSTOP autumn migration of shorebirds and Blackpoll Warblers from eastern North America to South America. Between Nova Scotia and New Jersey, thousands of birds take off on a 2,000-mile (3,200-kilometer), nonstop flight to the northeast coast of South America. The flight takes a minimum of about forty hours. By taking off after the passage of a cold front with associated west or northwest winds, migrants realize very fast ground speeds. A warbler whose airspeed is 20 miles per hour (32 kilometers per hour) would have to fly for a hundred hours to reach South America, which is virtually impossible. With a 30-mile-per-hour (48-kilometer-per-hour) tailwind, however, the

The tiny Blackpoll Warbler makes a two- to three-day nonstop flight across open ocean from eastern North America to South America. Strong westerlies and the northeast trade winds help push them to their winter habitat. They return to their breeding grounds by a more westerly route, because in spring they would encounter headwinds over the Atlantic.

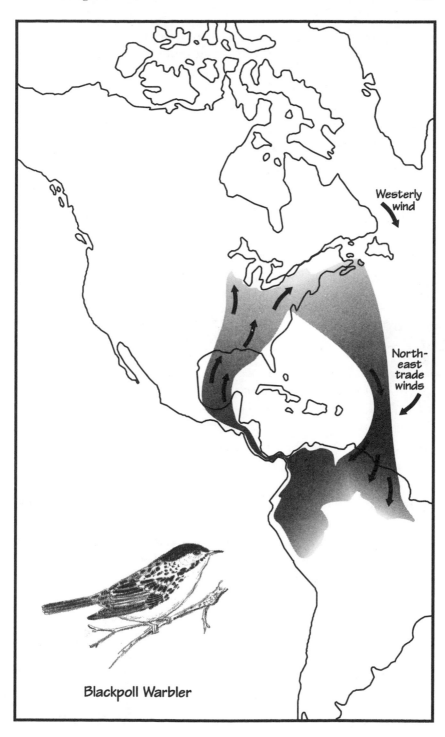

Westerly
wind

North-
east
trade
winds

Blackpoll Warbler

same migrant can realize a 50-mile-per-hour (80-kilometer-per-hour) ground speed. Passage time would then be forty hours. By flying southeast toward 125 degrees, the migrants can use westerly winds until they are beyond Bermuda. At this point they cannot return to land. As they continue south or southeast, they encounter northeasterly tradewinds of 10 to 20 miles (16 to 32 kilometers) per hour, which help them to the South American coast. When the warblers leave the Northeast coast, they weigh more than 20 grams. By the time they reach South America, they have lost 8 to 10 grams, mostly fat. These birds are visible to radar while flying at more than 5,000 feet above the ocean and over Bermuda and Puerto Rico. Some researchers and birders believe that this flight is initiated as far south on the Atlantic coast as New Jersey, but others are skeptical that Blackpoll or other warblers survive the flight. ■

CASE STUDY	*Golden Plovers Cross the Pacific.*

ALTHOUGH FEW BIRDS MIGRATE ACROSS THE VASTNESS OF THE PACIFIC Ocean, the Golden Plover, Bar-tailed Godwit, Ruddy Turnstone, Wandering Tattler, and Sharp-tailed Sandpiper fly over large portions of it. Golden Plovers fly from several Pacific islands to Alaska—a nonstop flight from Hawaii of more than 2,400 miles (3,800 kilometers). Studies done on Wake Island in the north-central Pacific show that Golden Plovers may fly more than 3,000 miles (4,800 kilometers) nonstop or in several jumps. These birds deposit massive amounts of fat, sometimes doubling their normal weight. One study demonstrated that they could fly nonstop for 5,000 miles (8,000 kilometers), an incredible flight for a bird that weighs only 175 grams. Golden Plovers also fly from eastern North America to South America in autumn. Similar flights are made by Ruddy Turnstones, a species that associates with Golden Plovers. Turnstones have been recovered in the Marshall and Caroline islands of the South Pacific only thirteen to forty days after being banded in the Pribiloff Islands near Alaska. This flight of 3,500 miles (5,600 kilometers) is probably done in several jumps. ■

TRANS-SAHARAN MIGRATION

At least a hundred species of European and Asian migrants, including songbirds, shorebirds, cranes, waterfowl, and raptors, winter south of the Sahara Desert. We know that some species fly east or west of the Sahara, thereby avoiding its inhospitable vastness. Many of these southbound birds bypass the long Mediterranean Sea crossing by flying across the Strait of Gibraltar or via the Middle East land bridge, especially Israel.

Those birds that do not fly around the Sahara must make stopovers or fly more than 1,400 miles (2,300 kilometers) nonstop. A controversy has developed as to which strategy migrants use. In one camp, sometimes called the British camp, are those who believe that many of the migrants, especially songbirds, fly thousands of miles without stopping from southern Europe to central Africa. This flight includes the crossing of the Mediterranean Sea and is comparable in length to the flight of North American migrants over the western Atlantic Ocean. In the German camp are researchers who are finding that many migrants stop over in the desert during daylight hours. Some individuals probably cross nonstop, but the species and numbers that do are unknown.

The Sahara is not the easiest place to conduct migration research, but in the last decade several German biologists have conducted excellent studies of stopover ecology of migrants at oases in Egypt and elsewhere. It is now known that after completing the Mediterranean crossing, many songbirds land in North Africa to forage and rest. They then finish crossing the Sahara, either by direct flight or by making shorter, one-night flights interspersed with daytime stopovers.

Several researchers from the Max Planck Institute in Germany have studied migrants along the Mediterranean coast of Egypt and at oases more than 100 miles (160 kilometers) to the south. They concluded that most birds do not cross the Mediterranean and the Sahara in one jump; instead, autumn migrants arriving at the Egyptian coast land before dawn and cross the Sahara later. Researchers also counted thousands of migrants shortly after dark in northern Egypt, indicating that the birds take off from sites a few miles to the north of the desert study sites. Since the birds spotted at night were European species that had made stopovers on the coast of Egypt after crossing the Mediterranean during a previous night, they had to have made at least a one-day stopover in northern Egypt before setting out over the Sahara. On days after nights when many birds were aloft, there were more birds in the oases. At one site more than a thousand birds of twenty-eight species were captured for banding at an artificial oasis made by "planting" a few fresh branches of eucalyptus and other trees in the desert. It appears, then, that many species of birds do make stopovers along the northern coast of Egypt as well as at desert oases.

Other researchers working in the western Sahara have also found many migrants at oases. Some of the species observed making stopovers were the Yellow Wagtail, Olivaceous Warbler, Garden Warbler, Subalpine Warbler, Willow Warbler, Pied Flycatcher, Spotted Flycatcher, and Chiffchaff. Especially interesting was the discovery that birds that normally rest in shrubs or trees were resting in the shade of rocks in the desert, presumably to avoid dehydration. It is likely that many birds make stopovers in the Sahara as a normal part of their migration.

The Sahara is not the only desert that represents a barrier to migrants: the Gobi in northern China, the Sinai in the Middle East, and the Atacama in Peru all pose dangerous crossings for migrants. A team of researchers from Hebrew University of Jerusalem and Tel Aviv University studied stopovers made by songbirds migrating through the Sinai in both spring and autumn. Their study site was a monastery built around an oasis. By banding Willow Warblers, Red-backed Shrikes, Blackcaps, and Redstarts, they found that only about 20 percent of the migrants stayed for two days or more and that the estimated stopover duration for all birds was between one and five days. About 80 percent continued their migration the night after they had arrived. Stopovers were shorter in spring than in autumn and shorter during late spring than early spring, suggesting that migrants are in a greater hurry in spring than in autumn. Because the majority of birds did not stay longer than one day, stopovers in the desert may be not for replenishing of body fat but for resting and avoiding the heat of the day, since daytime flight over the desert would accelerate evaporative water loss and lead to dehydration.

BARRIERS AND THE EVOLUTION OF BEHAVIOR

Barriers are probably a strong selective force in avian evolution. Certainly natural selection would favor those birds that can eat enough to fuel themselves for a long, nonstop flight, or those that know not to attempt such a crossing and fly around instead, or those that choose the shortest, quickest way over. But before we can say that barriers are a selective force that has changed bird behavior, two requirements must be met.

First, the behavior must have a genetic basis, because that is what natural selection acts upon. Most researchers presume that migratory behaviors have some genetic component (see chapter 10). Second, the selective force must act consistently over many generations. Barriers to migration satisfy this requirement because most have not changed for millennia.

Because evolution by natural selection takes many years—usually thousands of years pass before changes in body shape or behavior become obvious—we cannot observe the actual process of evolution, unless it is accelerated by a catastrophic event. Instead, we study the product of evolution and then attempt to infer what selective pressures were involved. In the case of barriers to migration, we see the behavior of birds that has already been shaped by natural selection.

While studying the spring arrival of songbirds that had flown the Gulf of Mexico, I was fortunate enough to observe what I believed to be natural selection at work. Walking the beaches of Horn Island off the coast of Mississippi, I found dozens of carcasses of trans-Gulf migrants, particularly large songbirds like Scarlet Tanagers, thrushes, Rose-breasted Grosbeaks, Yellow-billed Cuckoos, and even a Lincoln's Sparrow. All these birds weigh more than one ounce (30 grams) when they are in good condition. I also found feathers in the tide line and surf—small feathers, mostly from small birds like vireos, flycatchers, gnatcatchers, and warblers. It appeared that these small migrants die in large numbers. Counts of more than a thousand flight feathers in a few yards of beach were not unusual. Multiplied by hundreds of miles of Gulf coastline, these thousands of feathers indicate that millions of birds die each year while attempting the trans-Gulf crossing. The magnitude of this crossing, then, is quite likely a selective agent. Birds that do not have the strength or energy to complete the flight die.

One of the most spectacular reports of migrant mortality comes from the Mediterranean coast of Israel. A representative of the Society for Protection of Nature in Israel reported that more than a thousand raptors of at least twelve species were drowned in one day, including 826 Common Buzzards, 312 unidentified buzzards, 4 Long-legged Buzzards, 6 Black Kites, 3 Short-toed Eagles, 7 Lesser or Greater Spotted Eagles, 4 Booted Eagles, 4 Tawny Eagles, 124 unidentified eagles, 1 unidentified harrier, 2 Eurasian Kestrels, 8 European Sparrowhawks, 8 Griffon Vultures, 8 Egyptian Vultures, 8 unidentified raptors, and many other nonraptorial soaring birds. Whether these birds were attempting a water crossing or were blown out to sea by strong winds is unknown, but in either case, this incident shows that large bodies of water are strong selective forces. Mortality of this magnitude is probably the reason relatively few hawks and other soaring birds attempt long water crossings.

Smaller-scale mortality involving fewer individuals occurs regularly but is not predictable enough for researchers to study. It is likely that high mortality occurs every year along the Gulf of Mexico. Every year birders in the Dry Tortugas, small islands off the southwestern tip of Florida, report thousands of weakened migrants. Researchers have documented significant numbers of emaciated birds arriving in Louisiana and Mississippi during spring. Thrushes that usually weigh more than 30 or 35 grams with a normal amount of migratory fat arrive there weighing only 22 to 24 grams. How many exhausted thrushes and other birds fall into the Gulf before reaching southern Louisiana? The low body weight of the birds that do survive the crossing suggests that the flight is debilitating for many individuals and fatal for others. Does an emaciated Gray-cheeked Thrush weighing only 23 grams have as great a chance at survival and reproduction as one weighing 28 grams? Probably not. Thus, natural selection can work through either mortality or debilitation of individuals.

In the last three millennia, man has changed the nature of barriers to bird migration. The Sahara Desert has grown because of man's land-use practices. Desertification of the Sahel, a vast arid grassland and savanna south of the Sahara, is mostly a result of drought, cutting trees for firewood, overgrazing by cattle, and browsing by goats. The Sahara now constitutes a larger barrier for migration and also may have fewer stopover sites available. Will this change result in higher mortality among European migrants—or has it already?

Although the oceans, seas, and lakes have not changed in size in recent times, the habitats along their edges have changed. Migrants crossing a barrier now face degraded or changed habitats at both ends of their journey. A bird preparing to land in the coastal cheniers of Louisiana, for example, finds fewer places to rest and forage than fifty years ago because some forests have been cleared and in others the understory has been trampled and overgrazed by cattle. To the north, much of the coast is marsh; here migrants may have to fly still farther to find suitable habitat. The same thing has happened in the Northeast, where urbanization has encroached upon the coastal forests between Maine and Virginia, and in the Midwest, where farming has cut into the native grasslands and wetlands. With fewer places for birds to make stopovers, barriers to migration are growing larger.

Eight

Migratory Rest Stops

Picture yourself preparing to drive from Halifax, Nova Scotia, to Brownsville, Texas, and then on to Panama. You would have to drive for a week or more, making stops to sleep, eat, and refuel your car. Birds face some of the same problems as human travelers, and more. Without food and safe resting places, they cannot complete migration—and they will die. Migration is particularly challenging because the birds must meet their needs in strange, new habitats. A Pectoral Sandpiper that was hatched on the Canadian tundra, for example, may not have seen a tidal mudflat prior to arriving on the Atlantic coast in autumn; neither has a Blackburnian Warbler fledged in a boreal coniferous forest ever encountered a swamp forest of red maple and gum trees. Both must use such foreign habitats during migration. And these species will encounter new predators.

Stopover ecology can best be understood by examining three related processes: habitat selection, stopover duration, and weight change.

CHOOSING A PLACE TO LAND

After a night or day of migration, birds must make several decisions, the most important of which is choosing a hospitable place to feed and rest. Often migrants descend into hostile habitats, perhaps because they do not see well enough at night to judge the terrain correctly. Grebes and loons have been known to land in railyards, probably mistaking them for lakes because their flat expanses of black cinders make them look like bodies of water. This is a fatal mistake for these waterbirds, which can take off only from water. Similarly, cornfields, parking lots, and marshes are not good stopover habitats for forest-dwelling migrants. A Brown Creeper that finds itself 50 miles (80 kilometers) off the Atlantic coast after an October night of migration must return to shore and find a forest. Nevertheless, I have seen these birds resting on jetties and in dune grasses— inappropriate and unacceptable habitats. Although they offer a degree of shelter in which to rest, such sites have no food and little cover to protect Brown Creepers from gulls and other predators.

| CASE STUDY | *Night-Migrating Songbirds Select Stopover Sites at Dawn.* |

BECAUSE MANY SONGBIRDS MIGRATE AT NIGHT, THEY HAVE PROBLEMS finding suitable habitat in which to make stopovers. Birds frequently land in bizarre places—a thrush in a cornfield, for example. For songbirds that land before daybreak, the gray light of dawn and the first two hours thereafter appear to be the time when stopover habitat is selected. At this time some birds engage in what is termed morning flight.

A group of professional birders from the Cape May Bird Observatory studied morning flight in Cape May to determine which species undertook morning flight and at what time they did so. Among those that made morning flights were such Neotropical migrants as Blue-gray Gnatcatchers, twenty-some species of warblers, some vireos, orioles, tanagers, grosbeaks, and many non-Neotropical migrants, such as kinglets, Yellow-rumped Warblers, and many sparrows. Conspicuously underrepresented among the Neotropical migrants were Veeries, catbirds, cuckoos, and Gray-cheeked, Swainson's, and Wood thrushes. The study may be one of the first to use flight identification of the nearly indistinguishable fall warblers and other songbirds. Nearly 90 percent of the birds observed flew in the first two hours after sunrise. Despite the fact that these migrants were southbound in autumn, most flew north. After leaving the tip of the peninsula, they dispersed to the north of Cape May, where larger forests and more habitat are available. The purpose of morning flight therefore seems to be finding suitable stopover sites. ■

| CASE STUDY | Songbirds Compete for Food at a Stopover along the Gulf of Mexico. |

WORKING IN THE SMALL DUNE FORESTS, CALLED CHENIERS, OF COASTAL Louisiana, a pair of researchers confirmed food-based competition among songbirds. Wire cages were constructed on portions of trees to prevent warblers, vireos, and other songbirds from eating butterfly and moth larvae that were feeding on hackberry trees. This experiment permitted researchers to compare the number of larvae inside and outside the exclosure devices to determine whether migrants depleted food resources. They did: on the branches without exclosures, larvae were less numerous. Reduced prey in an area frequented by thousands of hungry migrant songbirds makes foraging more difficult and more competitive and reduces the quality of the habitat for late-arriving birds. ■

| CASE STUDY | Songbirds Quickly Select Habitat on a Mississippi Barrier Island. |

AFTER MAKING A 600-MILE NONSTOP FLIGHT FROM CENTRAL AMERICA to the United States each spring, millions of songbirds cross the northern coast of the Gulf of Mexico. Upon reaching the shore, many lean and hungry migrants descend to seek habitat in which to rest and feed. Their behavior is best described as frantic. Migrants fly a short distance, then land and fly again. They have not yet selected habitat but appear to be sampling what's available. There are six habitat types to choose from, but of about one thousand migrants observed, half were seen in just one. This habitat type represented only 6 percent of the island's total area and less than 10 percent of its vegetated area. The habitat of choice had a canopy of pine and a thick understory of shrubs. Structurally the most diverse habitat on the island, it was somewhat impenetrable. Some species of birds used the taller trees and others used the brush layer. Only a very small portion of the island was good habitat for these birds, which were selective and did not use just any habitat. ■

CASE STUDY	*Cryptic Connecticut Warblers Are Stopover Habitat Specialists.*

VETERAN BIRDERS KNOW THAT CONNECTICUT WARBLERS ARE SELDOM seen. Birders who do get a glimpse of this species are usually frustrated by fleeting and unsatisfying views. In a study done in Cape May, Connecticut Warblers were found to be very cryptic and habitat-specific. Researchers walked more than eighty transects in two autumn migration seasons but saw fewer than ten individuals of this species. The transects were walked along hedgerows, forest edges, open fields, and forest interiors. During a banding study in an adjacent hedgerow, field, and forest, however, about fifty-five individuals of this cryptic species were captured in just one autumn season. More than 95 percent of these birds were caught in four mist nets that had been set perpendicular to the hedgerows. Eighteen other nets placed in forest interior, forest edge, and open field captured very few Connecticut Warblers. Other habitat specialists were also found. More than 90 percent of the thrushes captured, and all of the Louisiana Waterthrushes, were taken in nets inside the forest. From these results, it's apparent that researchers sampling habitats to find certain species should combine visual observations and netting. Both banding and visual methods are biased when used alone. ■

Some types of habitats attract and support more species and more individuals than do others. This fact has implications for both the preservation of habitat and the management of open space for migrants, and the Western Hemisphere Shorebird Reserve Network is one group that seeks to identify and save the best habitats for migratory birds.

In the 1970s several shorebird biologists recognized that migrating shorebirds aggregated by the tens or hundreds of thousands at certain sites around the world. In North America Mono Lake in California, the Cheyenne Bottoms in Kansas, the Bay of Fundy in Nova Scotia and New Brunswick, and the Delaware Bayshore of New Jersey and Delaware are now recognized as crucial to the survival of migrants. Along the Delaware Bayshore, more than a million shorebirds gather in spring. Pete Dunne of the Cape May Bird Observatory and several volunteers made the first airplane surveys of the Delaware Bayshore phenomenon. Later, Brian Harrington, Pete Myers, and the New Jersey Endangered and Nongame Species Program found that some of the birds return to the same beaches in two or more subsequent migrations. Dunne speculates that about a half million Least Sandpipers and other shorebirds, such as yellowlegs, dowitchers, and dunlins, use the marshes and mudflats behind the beaches. In the late 1980s Cape May Bird Observatory volunteers and staff found that tens of thousands of Sanderlings, Semipalmated Sandpipers, and several other species return to the Bayshore in late June through early September. During this postbreeding migration, these birds make stopovers to feed on mull crabs, other invertebrates, and perhaps even larval horseshoe crabs.

Although sites like the Delaware Bayshore are now recognized as globally important, the Western Hemisphere Shorebird Reserve Network has no regulatory power to protect the sites. Instead, it concentrates on educating citizens and government officials about the migratory needs of these sensitive species. As a result, the New Jersey Nongame and Endangered Species Program and other state agencies are now leaders in recognizing that the long-term survival of many species is linked to success during migration, and thus to the preservation of stopover sites.

REFUELING DURING MIGRATION

For most migrants, fat ensures successful migration because it provides fuel for flight as well as for weathering storms and stopovers in inhospitable locales. A warbler that must stop in a small copse of trees in the middle of farmland probably will not be able to find much food, but its fat reserves will allow it to continue migration the next night. Those same fat reserves also provide resources for keeping the bird warm and avoiding starvation if it must stay several days in that habitat.

Some migratory birds put on enormous fat deposits during migratory stopovers. Turn-of-the-century shorebird shooters described Eskimo Curlews as being so fat the skin burst when a bird was shot; they called the curlews "doughbirds." Red Knots and Blackpoll Warblers are two of the many long-distance migrants that can come close to doubling their weight during migratory stopovers. A lean Blackpoll weighs about ½ ounce (12 to 13 grams). A fat one weighs more than 20 grams. This fat is used to make the marathon flight from the coast of New England to the north coast of South America during autumn migration, a trip believed to take forty to seventy hours, nonstop.

Fat is a rich source of energy, but how far a migrating bird can fly on a gram of fat depends on the size of the bird. Smaller migrants can fly farther per gram of metabolized fat than larger migrants. A Kentucky Warbler that weighs only ½ ounce (15 grams), for example, can fly more than 120 miles (200 kilometers) on a single gram of fat. It probably burns 1 or 2 grams of fat during a one-night flight. During a 600-mile (1,000-kilometer) nonstop crossing of the Gulf of Mexico, this bird might use 4 or 5 grams of fat and lose as much as 20 to 35 percent of its body weight during a 15- to 18-hour period. Tailwinds reduce energy consumption by nearly half, to 2 or 3 grams. Imagine how much fat would be required if the warbler experienced a headwind.

The relationship between flight distance and fat consumption has been determined mostly by theoretical means and is expressed in mathematical formulas that describe the energy cost of flight. Many books and papers on this topic have been published, and there's even a computer disk that can be used to simulate the migratory flight of birds, along with concordant weight loss. The calculations enable scientists to determine the flight range of migrants based on body weight and available fat, and thus to understand their energy needs, especially for species that require special habitats. Shorebirds migrating over the interior of a continent devoid of mudflats, riverbanks, wet meadows, or marshy areas must make stopovers in small but crucial areas. The Cheyenne Bottoms in Kansas and Mono Lake in California are two examples of stopover sites surrounded by inhospitable habitat. At the Cheyenne Bottoms, shorebirds congregate in the hundreds of thousands on their flight between Latin America and their tundra breeding sites. Birds that miss these threatened and shrinking sites will not find suitable habitat for hundreds of miles.

| CASE STUDY | *White-rumped Sandpipers Rest in Kansas during Spring Migration.* |

THE WHITE-RUMPED SANDPIPER IS ONE OF MANY SPECIES THAT USE THE Cheyenne Bottoms of Kansas as a staging and stopover site during spring migration. By late May more than a hundred thousand white-rumps have arrived there for a stay of one to two weeks. During this time birds gain 15 to 30 percent in weight, at a rate of about 2 percent of their arrival weight per day—the same as if a 150-pound (69-kilogram) man gained 3 pounds (1.5 kilograms) every day for two weeks. Brian Harrington of the Manomet Bird Observatory calculated that White-rumped Sandpipers with maximum fat accumulations have flight ranges in excess of 2,000 miles (3,200 kilometers). These birds can fly more than 100 miles (160 kilometers) on a single gram of fat; tailwinds can extend the range hundreds of miles. Because so many shorebirds use the Kansas site to refuel for their arduous flight to the tundra, changes to the habitat threaten shorebird populations. ■

| CASE STUDY | *Horseshoe Crab Eggs Feed Northbound Red Knots on the Delaware Bayshore.* |

RED KNOTS HAVE ONE OF THE LONGEST MIGRATIONS IN THE WESTERN Hemisphere: they breed in the Canadian Arctic and winter near Tierra del Fuego in southern South America, making a round trip of more than 18,000 miles (29,000 kilometers). Each spring, more than a hundred thousand Red Knots visit the Delaware Bayshore of New Jersey and Delaware to gorge on freshly spawned horseshoe

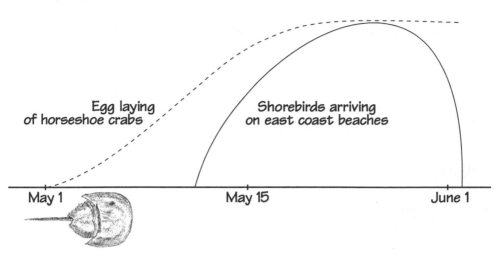

Many shorebirds time their spring migration stopovers to coincide with egg laying by horseshoe crabs. The eggs provide rich food in enormous quantities for Red Knots, Ruddy Turnstones, Semipalmated Sandpipers, and Sanderlings en route to the Canadian Arctic from South America; in two weeks the birds can gain half again their body weight in fat.

crab eggs. The spectacle is one of the wonders of the natural world and includes hundreds of thousands of Sanderlings, Ruddy Turnstones, Semipalmated Sandpipers, and Laughing Gulls. In a 1984 *Natural History* article shorebird biologist Pete Myers referred to this phenomenon as "sex and gluttony on Delaware Bay." During their mid- to late-May stopovers Red Knots stay about ten days and gain 40 to 50 percent of their body weight in fat. Weight is 120 to 130 grams on arrival, and 185 to 200 grams or more on departure— enough fat reserve to enable them to fly nonstop from the Delaware Bay to their arctic breeding sites. Using colored leg bands, Brian Harrington has documented that the knots make the trip from southern Brazil to New Jersey in an amazing eleven days: they do not make stopovers of significant duration during this part of their migration. In autumn many Red Knots fly nonstop between Nova Scotia or Massachusetts and the northern coast of South America. Color-marked knots sighted at James Bay, Ontario, have been resighted in Surinam in South America twenty-three days later. Birds marked in Brazil have been resighted only thirteen days later in

New Jersey, 5,000 miles (8,000 kilometers) away. The flight range of Red Knots may be greater than 3,000 miles (4,800 kilometers). In the Old World, the Siberian race of the Red Knot is also a long-distance migrant. Returning from Africa in mid-May, knots in West Germany average about 130 grams. Two weeks later the birds weigh about 190 grams, a gain of about 45 percent of body weight. ∎

| CASE STUDY | *White-crowned Sparrows Gain Weight at a Feeder in Maine.* |

THE WHITE-CROWNED SPARROW IS A CHUNKY BIRD THAT MIGRATES from northern mainland Canada to the central and southern United States. An undergraduate student at Bowdoin College in Maine captured dozens of these sparrows at a feeder in Maine during their southbound migration. He showed that of the white-crowns that stopped over for more than one day, the average stopover was three to four days. Most of his birds gained weight, usually at a rate of about 3 to 4 percent per day, for a total weight gain of more than 10 percent. ∎

| CASE STUDY | *Hummingbirds Stop Over at Feeders to Refuel.* |

SMALL BIRDS REQUIRE A TREMENDOUS AMOUNT OF ENERGY JUST FOR maintenance. Nevertheless, several species of North American hummingbirds make very long migrations. Weight gain by Rufous Hummingbirds was studied at a stopover site in the California Sierra Nevada by University of California at Irvine researchers. Birds were captured, weighed, and given markings of surveyor's tape. Birds were reweighed either by recapture or on a perch scale. On arrival they weighed 3.4 grams; just before departure they weighed about 4.7 grams. Some of these birds stayed as long as twenty days, although weight gain occurs in as little as four or five days. During the period of rapid weight gain, these dynamos deposit as much as ¼ gram per day. This means the birds increase their weight by 30 to 35 percent, or about 8 percent per day. ∎

Songbirds, too, must find high-quality habitat if they need to refuel before continuing their migration. A team of researchers from the University of Southern Mississippi found that migrants' use of sites in western Louisiana and on barrier islands along the Gulf coast of Mississippi varied according to several factors. Following trans-Gulf migration in spring, millions of North American songbirds representing fifty-odd species descend into coastal forests from Texas to Florida. The number of birds that stop over in the coastal forests of Louisiana depends on the weather. With thunderstorms or north winds, thousands of migrants drop from the sky. With southerly winds, conditions are favorable for onward migration and only a few migrants stop. The researchers also learned that migrants that stop in favorable weather are more likely to be emaciated or thin than birds stopping in thunderstorms. The emaciated migrants have no choice: they must stop to rest and forage. Thin birds stop over for more than one day; birds that arrive in better condition depart on the night after they arrive.

Stopover length and weight gain were related. In Louisiana, birds that made stopovers gained weight quickly. Hooded Warblers, Kentucky Warblers, Ovenbirds, Worm-eating Warblers, Prothonotary Warblers, and Swainson's Warblers made stopovers of one to seven days, with an average of two days. These migrants gained 3 to 5 percent of body weight per day, mostly fat. Vireos and thrushes that stopped gained weight similarly. Northern Waterthrushes and Tennessee Warblers rarely made stopovers, perhaps because this site did not satisfy their habitat requirements.

Many of the same species stop on East Ship Island and Horn Island, both 11 miles (17 kilometers) off Mississippi. Birds stopping on these islands, however, were usually in poorer condition than those landing in Louisiana, with some not being able to continue. Most of those that landed on the islands left as soon as it got dark. Those that stopped over for one or more days rarely gained weight, as in Louisiana.

The difference in behavior and lack of weight gain of birds that land in Mississippi can be attributed to differences in habitat. The Louisiana forest is dominated by hackberry, with toothache tree and live oak. The understory is luxuriant with a great deal of honeysuckle. Mississippi forests, dominated by slash pine and shrubs, are not so lush and have tough, dry leaves and needles. Insects, especially succulent moth larvae, are abundant in Louisiana, but the Mississippi insects are hard-bodied—less digestible and lower in caloric value. Birds gain weight rapidly in Louisiana because high-energy, easily digested larvae are abundant.

Comparison of migrants in Louisiana and Mississippi makes for great science and conservation research. The difference in observed weight gain and stopover duration at these sites attests to the large variability in habitat that migrants encounter. If good-quality habitat is not available, even thin, weak migrants must fly on until they find adequate resources. If they are too thin or weak to continue, they will either starve or succumb to predators.

Even in tolerable habitats, many migrants do not gain weight during the first day of a stopover, as was the case in Louisiana. Swainson's Thrushes studied during autumn migration at a wooded site in Wisconsin, for example, usually lost a small amount of weight during the first day of a stopover. Thereafter they gained weight in preparation for the coming journey to the tropics of Latin America. It may be that birds like the Swainson's Thrush need to learn how to forage in a new habitat before they can take advantage of the resources there. Another possibility is that the birds' physiology must change to digest unfamiliar foods. Either would explain the lack of weight gain during the initial days of a migratory stopover.

What about soaring birds? Because they do not have to generate the enormous amounts of energy that powered migrants do, hawks and other soaring migrants do not need to store as much migratory fat as sandpipers, waterfowl, and songbirds. A hawk may store only 5 to 10 percent of its body weight in fat. Although some biologists have made outrageous claims about Swainson's and Broad-winged hawks, there is no evidence to support conclusions of fat deposits exceeding 30 to 50 percent of fat-free body weight. The only real studies of fat deposition in hawks are those done in James Gessaman's lab at Utah State University. By measuring electrical conductance of the bird's body, the researchers found that wintering and migratory kestrels and migrating Sharp-shinned Hawks deposited up to 10 to 12 percent of their body weight in fat. This supports the contention of banders at Cape May who found that Merlins and some other migrants deposit only small amounts of migratory fat.

Although the duration of migratory stopovers varies, it is safe to say that migratory songbirds of many species spend two to five days at a good site. Larger birds, such as Red Knots, Sanderlings, and other shorebirds, make longer stopovers where food resources are super-abundant. It is not unusual for Red Knots and White-rumped Sand-pipers to spend ten days to two weeks at one location before continuing their journey.

Foraging and resting are not the only considerations of birds making stopovers. Entering a strange habitat or area also presents an increased risk of predation. For a woodland warbler that has never seen a Peregrine Falcon, Merlin, or American Kestrel, lessons can be costly. Good habitat, then, also offers refuge from predators.

Predation risk can be higher where migrating hawks make stop-overs, usually near coastlines or peninsulas. Places like Falsterbo and Cape May are not places where migrants can forget to be vigilant. Lapses result in significant mortality of migrants. At such sites it is not uncommon for Peregrine Falcons, Cooper's Hawks, or Goshawks to take smaller birds or even smaller raptors, like Sharp-shinned Hawks, European Sparrowhawks, or kestrels (both American and Eurasian). Food is food!

CASE STUDY	*Bramblings in Sweden Prefer Safety to Food during Stopovers.*

AKE LINDSTROM OF THE UNIVERSITY OF LUND STUDIED THE BEHAVIOR of Bramblings at migratory stopover sites in southern Sweden. These finches, along with Chaffinches, formed large mixed-species flocks averaging 400 to 450 individuals while foraging in farmland inter-spersed with hedgerows and forests. European Sparrowhawks and Merlins prey on these birds in both field and forest, but predation rates were lower in the forests. There was, however, more food for the finches in the fields. Because Bramblings spent more time in the forests, they seemed to prefer safety to food availability. It seems that a slower migration is preferable to no migration at all. ■

THE MOLT AND ENERGY FOR MIGRATION

Like migration, growing new feathers requires lots of energy. When the two demands occur during a short period of time, the necessary energy may not be available. At these times a hierarchy of biological needs dictates which activity is more important. Migration often wins.

Each year birds undergo a complete or partial molt to replace worn feathers. Ideally, the molt takes place when the bird has no great energy demands from other aspects of its biology. For many songbirds, shorebirds, and ducks, the best time for a complete molt is right after the breeding season, before migration. Other species, including many hawks and owls, have an interrupted molt. Body feathers all molt after breeding, but with the onset of migration, the birds simply do not have the energy to complete their wing molt. Two ages of feathers are therefore visible in the flight feathers of adult birds during autumn and winter: some new, some old. Birds of the year, of course, have all new feathers.

For a few other species, molt occurs during a prolonged migratory stopover. The migration prior to this molt is called molt migration and, aside from waterfowl, is unusual.

CASE STUDY	*Eiders and Other Sea Ducks Migrate to Molt on the Beaufort Sea.*

ONE OF THE MOST DRAMATIC INTERACTIONS OF MIGRATION AND MOLT IS the molt migration of Oldsquaws, Surf Scoters, and eiders. After breeding, many male sea ducks leave their mates incubating on nests and fly to communal molting sites. Point Barrow in northern Alaska attracts hundreds of thousands of male King Eiders and thousands of scoters and Oldsquaws during July and early August. There the males undergo a molt that takes more than a month. This migration is distinct from autumn migration, although in some places molt migration is southward and accounts for a substantial portion of the southbound, postbreeding migration. Some molt migrations, such as that of male King Eiders, involve distances of more than 600 miles (1,000 kilometers). Females, on the other hand, molt before leaving the breeding grounds and do not make a molt migration. ∎

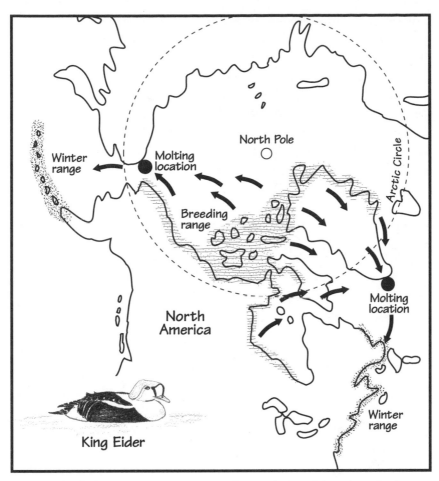

King Eider drakes migrate in two steps: first to their molting grounds, then to their winter habitat. Females molt at the breeding grounds and then proceed directly south.

CASE STUDY	*Yellow and Tennessee Warblers Molt While Migrating.*

MOST WARBLERS AND OTHER SONGBIRDS MOLT BEFORE MIGRATION, BUT Chris Rimmer at the Vermont Institute of Natural Science has found an interesting pattern in the Yellow Warbler. During southbound migration, this bird undergoes a molt and arrives at migration stopover sites with some old and some new feathers. This, then, is not really an interrupted molt but a continuing molt. Somehow these birds find the energy reserves during migration to complete their molt. Tennessee Warblers seem to have a similar molt pattern. Southbound Tennessee Warblers from Canada and northern New England arrive in central New York during late July, nearly a month before their arrival in Cape May, about 200 miles (320 kilometers) to the south. This means that Tennessee Warblers make prolonged stopovers after traveling only partway to their destination. Rimmer suspects this species, like the Yellow Warbler, has a way of dealing with molt and migration simultaneously. For a bird to molt at a migratory stopover, the habitat must provide food of sufficient energy and nutrients for both growing feathers and depositing migratory fat. ∎

Flight Speed and Distance

Should a migrating bird fly as fast as it can? By doing so, it will minimize the time needed to complete migration, but fast flight requires lots of energy. Many factors limit the speed at which a migrant can fly, so from a behavioral and evolutionary perspective the important question about flight speeds is not how fast migrants fly, but at what speed they can travel most efficiently.

Airspeed is the actual velocity that a bird flies with respect to the air. (The distance is in air miles.) With no wind a bird's ground speed—its speed with respect to the ground—and airspeed are the same. When a bird flies into a headwind, its airspeed is faster than its ground speed. When it flies with a tailwind, its airspeed is slower than its ground speed. Ground speed can be measured directly, but to determine airspeed, a researcher must measure the wind's speed and direction in addition to a bird's ground speed and direction, then add or subtract. Airspeeds and ground speeds are usually measured in meters per second (mps) or kilometers per hour (kph), but I have converted all speeds to miles per hour. To convert miles per hour to meters per second, divide miles per hour by 2.2. To convert miles per hour to kilometers per hour, multiply miles per hour by 1.6.

THE RANGE OF FLIGHT SPEEDS
Birds that use flapping flight during migration fly much slower than most people realize. It is safe to say that more than 90 percent of all

131

migrating birds fly at airspeeds between 14 and 45 miles per hour. Slower and faster flight speeds have been recorded, but they are exceptions.

The smallest birds fly slowest. Warblers, vireos, sparrows, wrens, and most other birds that weigh less than about 20 grams fly at airspeeds ranging from 10 to 30 miles per hour. Shorebirds, which may weigh as much as 200 grams, fly at airspeeds of 22 to 42 miles per hour. Waterfowl, still larger, fly as fast as or a little faster than shorebirds—between 28 and 50 miles per hour. There is a lot of variation among individuals and among species within these groups: some warblers lag behind others, and some ducks fly faster than other ducks. Size, structure, and physiology dictate the range of flight speeds among these birds.

Soaring migrants make better time in long, straight glides than when soaring in circles in thermals or other updrafts. During thermal soaring a small hawk's airspeed will be less than 12 miles per hour; larger hawks fly a little faster. In thermals these birds spread their wings and tails to nearly their maximum surface area, gaining lift but also increasing drag. The bird is trying to remain in updrafts, not achieve speed. When flying between thermals, on the other hand, these birds pull back their wings and fold their tails so that they increase their sink rate, reduce drag, and increase their speed. During gliding flight between updrafts, these migrants fly 20 to 45 miles per hour, although faster speeds have been recorded. Again, larger species generally fly faster than smaller species.

SELECTING A FLIGHT SPEED

Scientists who study bird flight rely on the highly mathematical theory developed by glider and powered aircraft pilots to determine what speeds are most efficient, but this degree of complexity is not needed to understand how birds select flight speeds. Most powered migrants are capable of flying at a fairly wide range of airspeeds, using a correspondingly wide range of energy. Energy is the price paid by the migrant for flying at different airspeeds. By dividing the speed by the amount of energy used, we determine the airspeed at which a bird travels the greatest distance. The speed that yields the greatest distance traveled for the amount of energy used is the best

FLIGHT SPEEDS OF MIGRATING BIRDS

The following flight speeds are estimates from radar studies of birds of similar size, and are measured in miles per hours. To convert to kilometers per hour, multiply by 1.6.

Songbirds	White-throated Sparrow	18–25 mph
	Black-and-white Warbler	15–23
	Northern Oriole	22–30
Shorebirds	Semipalmated Sandpiper	22–32
	Golden Plover	28–40+
Waterbirds	Scoters (Black and Surf)	26–50
	Common Loons	28–50+
	Double-crested Cormorants	25–38
	Canada Goose	32–42
	Red-breasted Merganser	33–44
Hawks	Broad-winged Hawk	30–44
	Osprey	32–46

speed for migrating when there is no wind—the maximum range airspeed. This is usually a few miles per hour faster than the airspeed at minimum power.

But that is for a world without wind. In reality, a migrant must choose from its range of possible speeds the best airspeed for the existing conditions. By flying at faster airspeeds in headwinds and slower airspeeds in tailwinds, a migrant can maximize the distance it travels. This strategy promotes a rapid yet energy-efficient migration. Presumably, the ability to employ this strategy evolved via natural selection; individuals that migrate less efficiently or less quickly produce fewer young for the next generation.

To determine whether birds make decisions about speed—correct decisions—we must observe their behavior during a wide variety of conditions, including headwinds and tailwinds. The theory that birds select good airspeed has survived tests by many researchers. Field studies have revealed slight aberrations, but overall most research supports the theory. And so the theory can be used to calculate the energy requirements and flight speed of birds during migration or foraging flights.

During autumn and spring hundreds of thousands of loons, sea ducks, brant, cormorants, and other nearshore seabirds migrate within a mile of the Atlantic coast near Cape May. Most of the birds fly within the first 150 feet of the surface. The speeds of hundreds of individuals were measured with stopwatches over a prescribed course. Speeds ranged from less than 20 to more than 44 miles per hour. With headwinds these birds fly at faster airspeeds and closer to the surface of the water than with tailwinds. Red-throated Loons averaged about 33 miles per hour—37 miles per hour with headwinds and 29 miles per hour with tailwinds. Loons, scoters, mergansers, Oldsquaws, and other species flew at similar speeds and made decisions about how fast to fly in a manner consistent with theoretical predictions. They flew at faster airspeeds with headwinds than with tailwinds. When migrants flew with tailwinds, ground speeds occasionally exceeded 50 miles per hour! Of interest is the fact that most species flew at speeds between the minimum power and maximum range airspeeds—something not predicted by mathematical models.

CASE STUDY	*Migrating Arctic Terns Fly High and Fast in Scandinavia.*

THE ARCTIC TERN MAY BE THE WORLD'S LONG-DISTANCE MIGRATION champion. Migration studies in Scandinavia with tracking radar revealed that during climbing flight over land, terns flew about 22 miles per hour. When they reached 3,300 feet, they averaged 31 miles per hour, slightly faster than the maximum range speed predicted for this species. A most interesting behavior was noted: terns flexed their wings, or drew them in slightly, as they flew faster, so that their wing structure and movement resembled those of shorebirds in flight. This is an example of how migrants make complex sets of simultaneous decisions involving changing speed, flapping kinematics, and wing planform—not unlike a jet pilot pulling in the flaps and changing speed with changes in altitude. ■

| CASE STUDY | *Migrants Select Airspeeds over the Swiss Alps.* |

SPRING MIGRANTS FLYING OVER THE ALPS FLEW FASTER INTO HEADWINDS than birds flying with tailwinds. Faster airspeeds used in headwinds improve the overall efficiency of flight, as predicted by aerodynamic theory. Nevertheless, there comes a time when birds cannot realize fast enough airspeeds to migrate efficiently. Few birds tracked in Switzerland migrated when headwinds exceeded 20 miles per hour, which made forward progress almost impossible. These findings are important because they show that birds can process considerable information about the speed and direction of the wind and make decisions that help them to migrate quickly and efficiently. The species involved were various thrushes, warblers, flycatchers, and several shorebirds (called waders in Europe) and waterbirds. The average airspeed for the songbirds was 28 miles per hour, and for the shorebirds, a few ducks, and rails, 33 miles per hour. ■

SELECTING A GLIDE SPEED
Because soaring birds alternate between soaring in a thermal and gliding to the next one, studying their behavior is tricky. During thermal soaring, they really do not select a speed that allows them to travel to a destination. Instead, they fly slowly so that they do not sink rapidly, thereby promoting fast ascent within thermals. Following a climb, they begin gliding in the direction of their destination. It is during the glide that speed selection occurs.

It would seem that a migrant should fly as fast as possible toward a destination, but if a bird glides too fast, it also sinks too fast, thereby making it necessary to find lift only a short time after starting a glide. Altitude is a gliding migrant's price, just as energy is the price for a powered migrant. A gliding bird wants to fly as far as possible during a given glide. The maximum glide ratio—the point at which airspeed divided by sink rate is greatest—is the best speed to use in still air with no thermals. When thermals are strong and abundant and lift is easy to find, a migrant should glide faster between thermals than when thermals are weak and scarce.

Flight altitude makes a difference in flight speed. A Swiss study showed that migrating hawks flew at slower airspeeds than hawks in Israel, New York, and Sweden. The Swiss hawks flew at less than 1,300 feet (396 meters) above the ground; the other migrants were seldom within 1,000 feet (305 meters) of the ground. These high-flying birds could afford to glide faster between thermals because they could rely on abundant and strong thermals to lift them back up. The fact that the alpine migrants flew at slower airspeeds is significant because it is exactly what the flight speed theory, outlined above, predicts. Recall that slower airspeeds are used by ridge-gliding hawks. Lower-flying birds should fly slower, and they do.

CASE STUDY	*Hawks Maximize Distance along an Appalachian Ridge.*

DURING AUTUMN MIGRATION THOUSANDS OF EASTERN HAWKS USE THE updrafts created by wind deflected off ridges and hills. Along the Kittatiny Ridge, home of such marvelous hawk-watching locations as Hawk Mountain Sanctuary in Pennsylvania, hawks glide continuously, sometimes for miles, in linear updrafts created by west and northwest winds. During this flight they often maintain a constant altitude with respect to the ridge, flying a few feet to several hundred feet above the ridgetop, depending on the strength and direction of the wind. Speeds used by these birds during ridge gliding varies. Using two-way radios and stopwatches, I measured the ground speed of migrants as they moved along a 300-yard section of Raccoon Ridge, New Jersey. When updrafts were weak, Sharp-shinned Hawks, Broad-winged Hawks, Ospreys, and Red-tailed Hawks flew at about 20 to 25 miles per hour. When updrafts were strong, these same species flew 28 to more than 35 miles per hour. The fastest speeds were realized during strong northwest and north winds. By maintaining a constant altitude over the ridge during this type of flight, the glide speeds used by these migrants approximate a distance-maximization strategy. That is, these birds make decisions that allow them to travel quickly and efficiently to their migratory goals. ■

| CASE STUDY | *Hawks Vary Their Glide Speeds.* |

THE MIGRATORY FLIGHT BEHAVIOR OF SEVERAL SPECIES OF HAWKS WAS studied in an Alpine pass in Switzerland with the help of a tracking radar. European Sparrowhawks and Common Buzzards changed their interthermal glide speeds to match the existing thermal conditions. Although they averaged 22 to 27 miles per hour, they flew faster with strong thermals than with weak ones. This conformed to the behavior predicted by theory. These airspeeds are slower than the speeds of Red-tailed Hawks, Ospreys, Broad-winged Hawks, and Sharp-shinned Hawks studied with tracking radar in central New York, and the Honey Buzzards, Sparrowhawks, and Lesser Spotted Eagles followed with a motor glider and radar in Israel. In central New York and Israel, interthermal glides were as fast as 36 to 50 miles per hour. Similarly, high-flying Common Cranes using partially powered glides between thermals flew at 34 to 50 miles per hour. These birds were followed with an airplane and tracked on radar during spring migration in southern and central Sweden. ■

The ability of hawks to use lift explains how soaring migrants can complete migration even though they fly slowly. The speeds of gliding migrants are slower than the speeds of powered aircraft and sailplanes. Sailplanes fly twice, sometimes three times as fast as hawks gliding between thermals, yet the hawks are able to migrate thousands of miles in a few weeks. This enigma is explained by aerodynamics. Hawks and other soaring birds may glide more slowly than sailplanes, but they use lift superbly. They are wonderfully adapted to exploit the smallest and weakest of thermals. They can turn on a dime, staying in the minutest area of lift. With this ability they can take off early in the morning and land late in the day, getting in more hours of flight on more days than sailplanes can. Finally, when thermals are not available, they do the one thing that sailplanes cannot do: they resort to powered flight until they find another source of lift.

DAILY FLIGHT DISTANCE
AND CROSS-COUNTRY SPEED

Knowing how fast migrants fly helps us learn how far they fly during a given flight. And by knowing how far migrants fly in a day or night, we can learn more about their habitat, foraging, and resting needs. Whether the flight is by day or night, I will hereafter refer to it as daily flight distance.

A researcher has several means of determining daily flight distance. The easiest is to multiply known flight speed (ground speed) times number of hours in flight. If a bird flies for eight hours per night at 25 miles per hour, it will realize 200 miles, assuming a straight course. Although this method is easy, it gives us only an approximation.

A slightly better method depends on the origin and destination of a given flight, whether for one day or several. If these facts are known, the average cross-country speed of a migrant can be determined. Cross-country speeds are usually slower than flight speeds because cross-country flights are seldom straight. Birds make turns and correct for errors in navigation and orientation.

Banding studies also reveal daily flight distances of migrants. A Sharp-shinned Hawk banded in the morning in Brooklyn was captured in Cape May after flying about 110 miles in seven hours, achieving a cross-country speed of 15.5 miles per hour. Another Sharp-shinned Hawk, banded in Cape May, was recaptured in coastal Virginia. It flew 140 miles in six hours for a cross-country speed of 23 miles per hour.

The best way to determine how fast migrants fly is to attach radiotransmitters to them. Assuming the transmitter does not affect the bird's flight, daily flight distance can be observed for several consecutive flights for a single bird. Few people have had the expertise, perseverance, and luck to use radiotelemetry successfully with migrating birds, however. Radiotelemetry has its drawbacks. The transmitter must not interfere with the bird's flight, inhibit flapping or other movement, or generate excessive drag as air passes over the bird's body. Most transmitters are designed to be less than 3 percent of a bird's mass. Since many birds can put on 20 to 50 percent of their body weight in migratory fat, this small amount of extra baggage is negligible.

But the miniaturization and design of transmitters are not the real problems; following radiotagged migrants with an automobile or a plane is. Researchers who use radiotransmitters go to such extremes as searching all night or all day for an elusive bird. They walk through forests and swamps at night, rent airplanes, and take great personal risks.

When successful, radiotelemetry tells us when a bird is migrating and when it is making a stopover. It also tracks the flight, which reveals how the bird makes decisions. The information gained from these studies is biased to larger migrants, however, because transmitters are still too bulky for shorebirds and songbirds and do not send a powerful enough signal for long-distance tracking. With further development, radiotelemetry techniques will offer the best method of studying migration.

CASE STUDY	*Songbirds' Cross-country Speeds Exceed Their Airspeeds.*

THE FLIGHT OVER THE GULF OF MEXICO FROM YUCATAN TO THE southern United States is a minimum of 600 miles for birds making landfall in southern Louisiana, northeastern Texas, or Mississippi. The distance is greater for birds that take off farther south or land farther inland. Birds are seen on radar arriving between 10 A.M. and noon at the northern Gulf coast have been flying for a minimum of 15 to 17 hours. These migrants realize a cross-country speed of about 35 to 40 miles per hour. Sometimes the birds do not arrive until late afternoon, in which case the cross-country speed would be slower. Still, these speeds are much faster than the airspeeds songbirds can attain— around 20 miles per hour—showing that the crossing is facilitated by tailwinds of about 20 miles per hour. With no tailwind the crossing would take thirty hours and many birds would not make it. With a headwind of 10 miles per hour, as with a cold front passing over the Gulf, the crossing could take sixty hours, in which case it would not be possible. ■

CASE STUDY	*Migrating Swainson's Thrushes Are Radiotracked in the Midwest.*

DESIGNING A RADIOTRANSMITTER FOR A THRUSH THAT WEIGHS LESS than 35 grams is tricky: the transmitter cannot weigh more than about 3 grams. William Cochran, the dean of American radiotransmitter research, followed a Swainson's Thrush fitted with such a transmitter for 950 miles during six nights of spring migration in the midwestern United States. Between Arkansas and Illinois, the thrush flew six nights for an average of seven hours of flight per night and a nightly distance of 66 to 234 miles. The average nightly distance was about 125 miles, for a ground speed of about 19 to 20 miles per hour. Following this and other species, Cochran learned that individuals differed greatly in their behavior and that birds sometimes land in unsuitable habitat during darkness. One thrush landed in a cornfield—imagine that. ■

CASE STUDY	*Colorado Bald Eagles Cover 125 Miles a Day.*

THE SAN LUIS VALLEY OF COLORADO HOSTS A LARGE WINTERING POPU-lation of Bald Eagles. Transmitters were affixed to several of these birds to study their spring migration. One bird was followed 1,230 miles in fifteen days to north-central Saskatchewan. It flew on only six days and was stationary for five days of inclement weather. This study—one of very few in which birds were captured in their wintering area and followed to their breeding site—shows that the entire spring migration of these individuals is brief, taking a little more than two weeks. The birds frequently flew more than 125 miles per day, although on many days they averaged only about 95 miles. One individual flew 125 miles per day in five consecutive flights, for a total of 625 miles. One of the most interesting observations was a reverse migration. After flying 92 miles on its first day of migration, an eagle flew into a snowstorm in the mountains. The next morning it turned around and flew back to its wintering site. It reinitiated spring migration several days later, when the weather was better. These daily flight distances are similar to those flown by recently fledged Bald Eagles followed between northern California and northern British Columbia during spring migration. ■

CASE STUDY	*A Sharp-shinned Hawk and Peregrine Falcon Lead Researcher on a Fall Odyssey.*

THE FIELDWORK OF BILL COCHRAN READS LIKE THE DIARY OF INDIANA Jones. He has followed migrating Peregrine Falcons out over the Atlantic, almost running out of fuel, and narrowly avoided arrest while trying to track Peregrines. But his reward is some of the best radiotelemetry work yet conducted. After radiotagging an immature female Sharp-shinned Hawk on the shore of Lake Michigan in Wisconsin, Cochran followed it for eleven days to Alabama. This bird flew in the migratory direction on nine of the eleven days: three to five hours of flight on each of four days, and six hours on each of four days. On day eleven he lost the bird. The average distance per day of travel was 94 miles, or nearly 21 miles per hour in cross-country speed. On some days the hawk flew less than 60 miles and on others it flew more than 125. An immature female Peregrine Falcon tagged by Cochran at the same site in Wisconsin flew to Mexico in only eleven days. This bird flew for similar time periods as the Sharp-shinned Hawk even though the Peregrine is a long-distance migrant and the hawk is a middle-distance migrant. The Peregrine also flew short precursor flights about half an hour before beginning migration. These flights were mostly oriented in the migratory direction, they were fairly slow, and they were at low altitudes. Perhaps they were hunting flights? ■

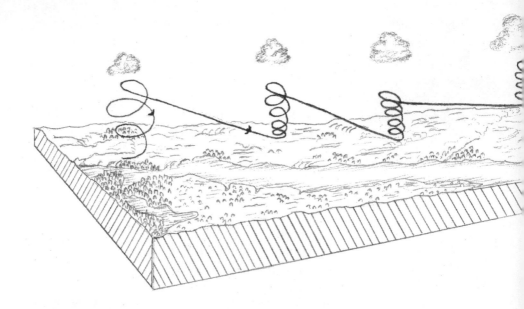

CASE STUDY	*Reverse-Migrating Canada Geese Fly 530 Miles Nonstop.*

SEVEN RADIOTAGGED CANADA GEESE WERE FOLLOWED BETWEEN THEIR breeding lake in southern Manitoba, Canada, and their wintering site in southern Minnesota. The geese often flew in an inappropriate direction for migration, a behavior often referred to as reverse migration and assumed to be exploratory in intent. Minimal flights of 170 miles were the rule, but nonstop flights by four birds exceeded 530 miles. Cross-country speeds during these longer flights averaged around 30 miles per hour. Reverse migration flights in spring were shorter than such flights in autumn, perhaps because prevailing winds in autumn were favorable. Flights of this length in the wrong direction are not that unusual among waterfowl and show how powerful these fliers are. ■

The latest development in radiotracking is the use of satellites. By equipping eagles, cranes, and other large migrants with solar-powered transmitters, scientists are now tracking these birds over

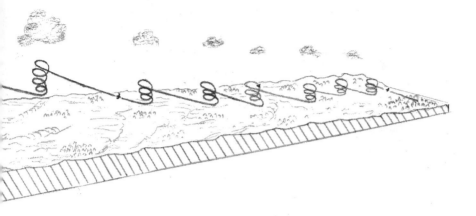

*From takeoff to landing, hawks and other
soaring birds can average about 25 miles per
hour—200 miles in an eight-hour day.*

thousands of miles between breeding and wintering sites. These
tracks promise to give us some of the best information on how birds
migrate.

Cross-country speeds of such soaring migrants as eagles average
about 25 miles per hour or less. This means they fly about 200 miles
in eight hours, although flight time is often shorter. Cross-country
speeds of powered migrants range from as little as 15 miles per hour
to as much as 40 miles per hour, depending on wind direction. Most
important is the role of wind. If birds have strong tailwinds, travel is
rapid; with headwinds progress is poor. Birds' strategy is to fly as long
as possible when winds are favorable, and not to fly at all when
winds are opposed to the migratory direction.

Finding the Way

TWICE EACH YEAR THE ENDANGERED KIRTLAND'S WARBLER MIGRATES between its breeding site in a small area of northern Michigan and its wintering area in the Bahamas. Since only a few hundred of its species remain, it's particularly important that the birds find their way back to the breeding area. If a bird doesn't make it to the precise locale, it won't find a mate, so a mistake of only a few miles out of 2,000 can remove that individual from the breeding population and bring the species closer to extinction. Fortunately, the Kirtland's Warbler, like most other migrants, has an uncanny ability to find its way home.

To fly into the unknown over inhospitable habitat takes great faith. How does a young bird that has never left its native habitat know where it is going or how to find its destination? For that matter, how does an adult that has already made a complete migration know where it is and remember where to go?

That birds find their way between breeding and nonbreeding sites, often over very long distances, implies that migrants have both a compass and a map. For birds, as for human travelers, both are necessary. The map tells the traveler where he is and where he is going; the compass allows him to go in a given direction

Orientation and navigation of migrants have been studied more than any other aspect of migration. Researchers use two approaches. The first involves observation of wild birds using radar, ceilometer, or direct visual methods (usually a hand-held compass). These methods have shown us that migrants can maintain straight courses through the air and that they possess some sort of internal compass.

The second approach involves controlled experiments or field trials with captive migrants. This approach is important because a researcher can control and manipulate the circumstances of an experiment and test birds under various conditions. By changing the cues available to a migrant, we may learn even more about avian orientation systems than we do from field studies.

Cages in which birds' orientation ability could be tested were first used in Germany in the 1940s. Researchers wanted to know whether birds could use the sun as an orientation cue. Cages had already been used to measure nocturnal migratory activity, or migratory restlessness. Birds ready to migrate hop from perch to perch for hours, and their activity pattern can be monitored. The orientation cages had eight perches, each capable of registering the number of hops in each of the eight cardinal directions—north, northeast, east,

The Emlen Funnel, with an ink pad at the bottom and blotter paper on the walls, tests the orientation of migrants. The restless Savannah Sparrow hops in the same direction it would fly.

southeast, and so forth. In the 1960s Stephen Emlen and his father, John Emlen, working at the University of Wisconsin, invented a different type of cage. They designed an inverted funnel of blotter paper with a mesh top through which the bird could see the night sky but not escape. The bird placed in the cage hopped, presumably in the migratory direction, on an ink pad placed at the center of the base of the inverted cone; the ink pattern indicated its directional preference.

The use of such cages revolutionized the study of orientation: orientation cages permit experimental manipulation. Using these devices, Stephen Emlen learned that Indigo Buntings were able to orient via the pattern of stars in the night sky. He did some of his experiments under a natural sky and others in the controlled environment of a planetarium. He changed the position of stars in an attempt to confuse birds, then observed how they responded. Since Emlen's seminal work, White-throated Sparrows, Savannah Sparrows, and Bobolinks have been tested in orientation cage experiments.

THE COMPASS

The migratory pathways used by birds are influenced profoundly by topography, geography, and wind. These routes are not always the same from year to year, although there are many sites along coastlines, mountain ridges, and peninsulas that are regular scenes of mass migration. Bodies of water, deserts, mountain ranges, and some other topographic or physiographic features of the earth can act as barriers to migration, or as leading lines that many migrants follow. That millions of migrants are seen along these leading lines shows they are important in orientation and navigation, as well as in the evolution of migratory behavior.

Several researchers have concluded that wind is one of the strongest factors in the evolution of migratory pathways, and that its role is enhanced by the presence of barriers. Sidney Gauthreaux's work has revealed a strong relationship between prevailing seasonal wind patterns and migratory directions by plotting both on the same map of North America. The correlation between wind direction and migratory direction in both spring and fall is striking. His maps also show that prevailing winds do not blow directly to or from migratory destinations. Migrants that flew a straight-line course between wintering and breeding sites would be inhibited by prevailing winds. Are these prevailing winds a strong enough selective force for birds to have evolved curved rather than straight pathways?

To answer this question, we need to compare great circle routes and rhumb-line courses. A great circle route takes advantage of the earth's curvature to find the shortest distance between two points, but it means changing flight direction continually. A rhumb-line route has a constant geographic bearing but is the longer distance between two points. (Although a rhumb-line migration course is along a constant geographic bearing, when plotted on a map, this route can appear as a curve because it goes over a sphere. The great circle route can appear to be a straight line when plotted on the sphere, even though this route requires a constantly changing bearing.) Many long-distance jet pilots rely on great circle routes, especially when they fly at high latitudes. To fly nonstop from Chicago to Moscow, for example, it is shorter and faster to fly northward, over the pole, than to go eastward across the Atlantic.

CASE STUDY	*Migrating Geese and Shorebirds Maintain a Constant Compass Bearing.*

Tom Alerstam, a Swedish biologist, has investigated great circle routes and concluded that these paths—the shortest routes for jet pilots—are not always the most efficient for migrating birds. In fact, migrating birds rarely use them. Alerstam and other biologists at the University of Lund found that Brant Geese, Ruddy Turnstones, and Red Knots fly rhumb-line routes from Iceland (a stopover site after leaving from Europe) to northern Canada and northwestern Greenland. The difference in compass bearing between a rhumb-line and a great circle route is 15 to 30 degrees, depending on destination. This is not a large difference, given the weak intensity and steep inclination angle of the magnetic field at high latitudes, which make it difficult to use magnetic cues for orientation. The flight is 1,000 to 1,500 miles long and requires more than forty hours to complete. A great circle route would have reduced the distance flown by about 5 percent. ■

A great circle route—any line that would cut the globe into two equal halves—is always the shortest distance between two points. But birds that migrate between Iceland and the Canadian Arctic fly the somewhat longer rhumb-line course—a constant compass bearing—during spring migration. The use of rhumb-lines by Red Knots, Ruddy Turnstones, and Brant Geese suggests that birds do indeed have innate compasses.

Greenland

Iceland

1,584 miles

1,665 miles

Canada

Some migrants do seem to use great circle routes, but wind and topography pose difficult, important problems. The correspondence between wind direction and migratory direction shown by Gauthreaux's maps suggests that many migrants have evolved downwind migratory pathways and that wind is a powerful selective force. The Swedish biologist Kai Curry-Lindahl also has suggested that long-distance migrants fly along curved flight lines, with the curves or ellipses being oriented in such a way that birds take advantage of prevailing winds to make better progress.

Wind and topography work together. In some places with strong winds, birds that fly downwind may have a distinct advantage. If it is autumn in a northerly latitude, for example, rapid downwind flight away from the colder center of a continent to a milder coastal area would be favored over slow progress in another direction. As they move away from the breeding range, the migrants may find more favorable winds and begin to cover immense distances in the correct direction. Prevailing winds seem to be part of the reason why so many migrants, including so many western species, are evident along the East Coast. Western Kingbirds, many warblers, and some scoters—including White-winged Scoters, which breed in Saskatchewan and Alberta—fly almost due east (90 to 120 degrees) in autumn to their wintering grounds along the Atlantic coast. After these migrants arrive on the mid- and southern Atlantic coast of North America, they are far more likely to find easterly winds, which would help them avoid being blown out over the Atlantic Ocean.

One of the prevailing theories of migratory orientation behavior is that some birds are deflected by the wind from some axis of migration or preferred direction of migration. This theory has become dogma, although few researchers have adequately tested or examined hypotheses that would allow it to be verified. In the 1930s a researcher proposed that many Sharp-shinned Hawks were seen along the coast because they had been pushed there by north and west winds. Later, a formalized theory of wind drift was proposed. Wind drift may push some birds to the coast, but other birds are attracted there. A bird heading south with a west wind will drift to the southeast. The distance it deviates from its heading course has been interpreted—perhaps incorrectly—as the amount of drift. The enormous aggregations of

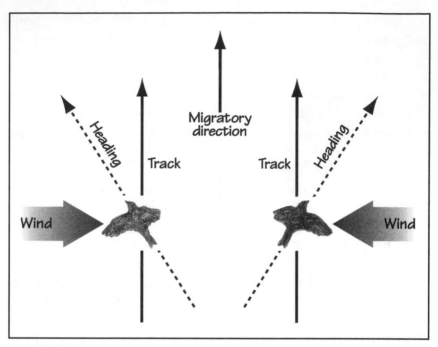

To maintain a constant track direction (the path over the ground) and reach its destination, a bird must change its heading (the direction it faces) into the wind.

songbirds and hawks that are seen along the Atlantic, for example, should not be considered a result of drift because some of these birds actually fly toward the coast, even against easterly winds.

Maintaining a straight course in the preferred migratory direction with a headwind or tailwind is easy: the direction a bird faces is the same as its resulting track over the ground. With a wind from the left or right of the migratory direction, however, a bird must compensate with a heading that is into the wind. If the difference between the track and the heading is correct, the bird will go the right way. If the difference is not enough, the bird will drift. To correct for drift, a bird must use some sort of landmark. Over land in daytime this is difficult only when the winds are strong. At night or over the sea, landmarks are not visible and waves move with the wind, making them unreliable gauges.

Because the land mass to the north and east of the mid-Atlantic coast is immense, the postbreeding migration southward inevitably brings a great number of birds to coastal areas like Cape May and the Outer Banks of North Carolina. These birds have not drifted here by mistake. For some species, such as Sharp-shinned and other bird-eating hawks, the coast is a giant cafeteria. With millions of immature songbirds and shorebirds looking for places to rest and forage, the pickings for a hungry raptor are easy. This may explain why so many raptors are counted along coastlines in autumn and why a majority of them are bird-eaters.

CASE STUDY	*Songbirds Follow the Hudson River in Autumn.*

RESEARCHERS FROM THE STATE UNIVERSITY OF NEW YORK AT ALBANY studied flight direction of night-migrating songbirds during autumn at two sites to see whether a river could be used as an orientation cue to correct for wind drift. The birds included warblers, sparrows, kinglets, and thrushes. Ceilometers were used to determine direction of migrants flying at a site on the Hudson River and at a location about 20 miles to the west, where birds could not see the river. With light winds or winds that were not westerly, both groups flew to the southwest. With westerly winds the birds inland flew southeast, and birds flying along the river followed it in a nearly southerly direction. This study seems to indicate that birds can and do correct or compensate for potentially drifting winds if topographic landmarks are present. Although our study seems to show that at times some songbirds follow rivers, the shoreline of the Hudson River south of Albany is lighted, so the birds may have cued not on the river but on the lights. We thought of asking everyone along the river to turn out their lights to test our idea . . . ■

Wind drift should not be entirely discounted, however, because some birds simply cannot compensate for strong winds. It is also likely that most daytime migrants correct for wind drift, which may occur more often among slower species, such as flycatchers, gnatcatchers, and others that weigh less than about 15 grams. In flight, these species are capable of correcting only for weak winds. Nocturnal migrants tend to be strong, fast fliers, and thus less likely to be drifted. Still, these birds must correct for drift.

Birds that are being drifted often do not have visual landmarks on which to set a course. Unlike nocturnal migrants and migrants flying over the ocean, far from land, daytime migrants can use landmarks to compensate for wind drift. Such topographic features as coastlines, rivers, and ridges act as leading or diversion lines for migrants. Hawks are seen most often at these leading lines, partly because they fly at relatively low altitudes near ridges and coastlines and partly because some utilize updrafts at these sites.

THE MAP

A bird's internal compass permits orientation in a given direction, but it does not reveal information about geographic location. The migrant also needs a map to determine its position and destination as well as identify landmarks along the way. The search for the map mechanism used by migrants, however, has been fraught with dead ends and several unsubstantiated hypotheses.

Many researchers who have attempted to find the navigation maps used homing pigeons as their model animal and suggested that birds rely on magnetic or olfactory cues. Though pigeons have been shown to have some ability to use such cues, they do so during homing flights, not migration. The elaborate hypotheses proposed for a map system have been difficult to test, and we are still waiting for research that uses actual migrants.

Peter Berthold of the Max Planck Institute has proposed a means by which birds could find their way during migration. Not strictly a map, the mechanism is a time-distance program, based on an innate compass bearing. The hypothesis was originally outlined in 1934 to explain how inexperienced birds found their way to and from their wintering grounds. More recently, it has been refined and named the *vector navigation hypothesis* by Klaus Schmidt-Koenig of the University of Tubingen.

The hypothesis states that birds have an innate time program coupled to an innate flight direction. Birds in their first migration—the young of the year—are thought to be genetically programmed to fly in a given direction for a given period of time. After doing so, they have arrived either at their destination or at a point where migratory direction changes. The innate directional information is programmed into all members of the population that uses a particular migration pathway.

For this hypothesis to be proven, both the time or distance a migrant flies and its direction of flight must be shown to be passed genetically from one generation to the next. And in fact, both have been demonstrated in elegant experiments and field data.

Some evidence for a genetic basis for the vector navigation hypothesis comes from the difference in directional preferences among European migrants, which use one of two routes into Africa: either southwest to cross the western Mediterranean into Africa, or southeast to Africa across the eastern Mediterranean or the Middle East. Both routes avoid a long crossing over the Mediterranean Sea and skirt the Italian peninsula, where birds have been killed for millennia. When young birds from eastern Europe are placed in orientation cages at night, they orient to the southeast. Birds from western Europe orient southwest. The average difference in migratory direction is about 50 degrees.

CASE STUDY	*European Blackcaps Use a Time-Distance Program.*

THE EUROPEAN BLACKCAP IS A SMALL SPECIES OF EUROPEAN WARBLER. Among its several populations are a population from northern Europe that migrates long-distance, and a group from southern Europe that migrates only a short distance. A pair of German researchers questioned whether migratory distance was programmed into an individual's genes. If it was, hybrid offspring from a cross between northern and southern parents would have intermediate migratory tendencies. The experimental breeding was done, and their suspicions were confirmed. Both parents and offspring were tested in activity cages to see how much the birds hopped. The amount of hopping was greatest in the northern, or long-distance, migrant Blackcaps; the least in southern, or shorter-distance, migrants; and intermediate in the hybrid offspring. That the offspring demonstrated intermediate migration tendencies strongly suggests that the time–distance portion of the migratory program of this species is genetically determined. ∎

| **CASE STUDY** | *A Time-Distance Program in European Garden Warblers Is Genetically Controlled.* |

THE AUTUMN MIGRATION OF BANDED GARDEN WARBLERS FROM GERmany to Africa is by way of Spain and Morocco. To reach Spain from Germany, birds must fly southwest toward about 230 degrees. After crossing into Africa, the birds change direction to due south (180 degrees), a difference of about 50 degrees. Are they genetically programmed to change direction after a certain number of days of orienting in one direction? To find out, researchers placed Garden Warblers that had been hand raised in orientation cages every night for an entire migration season. It was evident that the birds changed direction at about the correct time during the autumn migration. The change in direction from southwest to south corresponded to the dates when wild Garden Warblers were crossing into Africa. It seems, then, that Garden Warblers are genetically programmed to fly a given time and then change their migratory direction. ∎

| **CASE STUDY** | *European Starlings Demonstrate an Innate Directional Program.* |

MANY BIRDERS CONSIDER THE STARLING THE RAT OF THE BIRD WORLD, especially those of us who live in North America, where it is not native. In their native Europe, starlings make regular migrations. In the mid-1950s a Dutch scientist named Perdeck conducted what was to become a classic field experiment in animal migration using these

Garden Warblers appear to be programmed to fly southwest for a set period of time, then change direction to south, and finally head southeast to complete their migration from Germany to Africa.

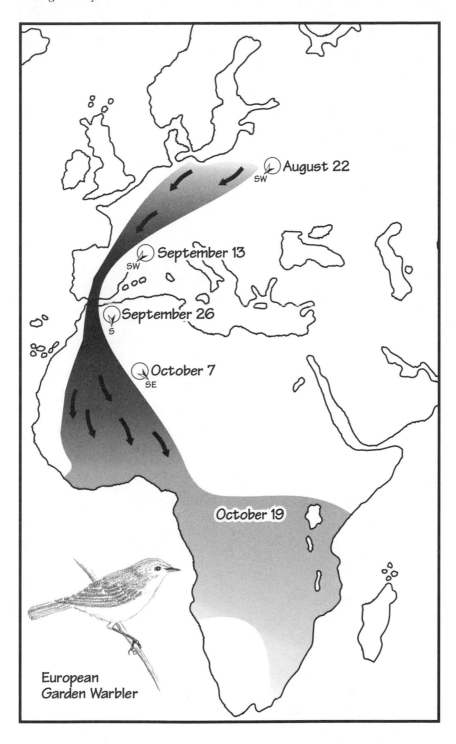

August 22
SW

September 13
SW

September 26
S

October 7
SE

October 19

European
Garden Warbler

birds. He captured and banded more than 11,000 adult and immature (first-year) starlings during autumn migration in the Netherlands
and transported them to Switzerland, where they were released. After
several months, information on recovery locations began to trickle in.
Most of the immature birds that were recovered were in southwestern
France and northern Spain. These individuals had continued their
migration in the same direction as those immatures banded and
released in the Netherlands. Adults, on the other hand, flew almost
due west toward the northwestern coast of France and some continued into England, where the species normally winters. These experiments showed that adults could truly navigate: they knew where they
were going and went there. Immature birds that had never migrated
seemed to have a time-distance program: they flew in a genetically
determined direction that did not change even after the birds were
transported to another location. Perdeck's results have become some
of the most important information ever gathered on bird migration. ■

Once a bird has completed its first migration successfully, it has a
rudimentary map. It knows where it has been and where it is. But
does it have a complete map? Probably not: the map is limited to
those pathways and places that the bird has experienced. Perhaps—
and this is an idea that has gained acceptance—a bird relies on a
three-stage orientation and navigation system. In the first stage a
bird orients toward a goal for a specific amount of time—the vector
navigation, or time-distance, program. Once it arrives within several
hundred miles of its destination, an innate map of magnetic or olfactory cues allows the bird to find its way to within a few miles of
home. That's the second stage. Finally, topographic features guide the
bird to its destination, whether it be a breeding or a wintering site.
This system works only after a bird has completed one migration
southward and therefore knows its destination at each end of the
journey. This experience enables success during future migrations.

The vector navigation hypothesis offers an adequate explanation
of the phenomenon for immature birds, but there are other models
for navigation programs. For species that migrate in flocks along traditional routes, young birds may acquire their knowledge of migratory routes and distances from adults that have made the trip

previously. This would constitute a cultural transmission of navigation maps. These birds must migrate in flocks.

THE CUES

By the early 1980s it had become obvious, at least in cage experiments, that birds were capable of using several cues to orient during migration, including the moon, the sun, the setting sun, the plane of polarized light (from the sun or setting sun), stars, wind, magnetism, topography, and olfactory cues. With so many possibilities, it is exceedingly difficult to study one cue in isolation from the others.

Although migrants have been shown to orient using star patterns, biologists are fairly certain that magnetism is the most important source of directional information for migrating birds. Researchers suspected magnetism early on, but because a migrant must have a very sophisticated compass to use this type of information, they did not study it. Magnetism was also difficult to study, since researchers needed to construct Helmholtz coils (giant loops of wire that simulate magnetic fields) and have magnetic detectors for the experimental chambers. Doubt about magnetism was rampant, even after two German researchers, Wolf and Roswitha Wiltschko, published evidence of a magnetic compass in European Robins and other birds in the early and mid-1970s. But slowly, the results of other researchers confirmed their findings.

Relying on work done by some of the earliest migration researchers, Frank Moore of the University of Southern Mississippi wondered whether migrants used the sun as an orientation cue. What was startling about this theory was that Moore suggested this for nocturnal migrants. Because night-migrating birds take off just after the sun sets, Moore reasoned that they probably set or calibrated their compasses at that time of day or shortly thereafter. Furthermore, he reasoned that because the position of the setting sun changed very little from day to day, it offered migrants a reliable source of information. In experiments using Savannah Sparrows, he found that the position of the setting sun was indeed the migrants' source of directional information.

More recently, researchers, including Moore, have proposed that it is not the location of the setting sun that is the cue but the plane of polarized light made by the setting sun. Some researchers now believe that the setting sun, or the plane of polarized light caused by it, calibrates migrants' compasses to such cues as star or magnetic compasses. This make good sense, as the birds take their cues just as they set off on a night flight.

CASE STUDY	*Savannah Sparrows Set Their Nocturnal Compasses by the Setting Sun.*

SAVANNAH SPARROWS ARE MIDDLE-DISTANCE, NOCTURNAL MIGRANTS that weigh less than 20 grams. When he tested these birds in both Emlen funnels and other cage devices, Frank Moore found that the location of the setting sun was an important orientation cue. The accuracy of orientation was best when the setting sun was visible. When sunset was obscured either by covers on the cages or by clouds, the accuracy of orientation was significantly reduced. His critical test was ingenious. He placed mirrors around the cage to alter the position of sunset. When sunset was shifted 90 degrees from the true sunset position, birds shifted their orientation 90 degrees in the same direction. ■

The discovery of a link between polarized light and magnetic cues is new. Experiments involving Savannah Sparrows from North America and Silvereyes from Australia revealed that birds may "see" magnetic fields. Although magnetism itself is invisible, birds can see the plane of polarized light and use it to calibrate their magnetic compass. Thus, part of the avian eye may be able to detect the earth's magnetic field. Although these results are preliminary, they provide insight into the complexity of a biological system and the enormous amount of work required to unravel its mysteries.

Today, migration biologists concur that birds use many sources of directional information during migration, including magnetism, olfactory (chemical) cues, the sun, sunset, and the stars. To read these cues, the birds use various organs as receptors. The eyes are undoubtedly important for sunlight, the plane of polarized light, and the stars. Chemoreceptors in the nose and associated neurological connections detect olfactory cues. Locations in the head or neck or both have been suggested for magnetism. The substance that acts as a magnetic compass or transducer has also been elusive. Magnetite (an iron substance), melanin, photopigments, and others have been candidates. Parts of the ophthalmic nerve, which reads visual cues, in the upper beak and head area of Bobolinks are responsive to magnetic stimulation. Both iron oxide and melanin are present there, so these fibers are candidates for future studies. Undoubtedly, the organ with the ability to detect and use orientation cues is located in the head and brain, but beyond this it is still too early to say with any certainly which organ detects magnetism. Now that studies are revealing a relationship between polarized light and magnetism, the eye has become an important candidate.

Although it is now known that migrants use many cues, it is not obvious which of the cues is most important, whether there is redundancy in the system, and which cues are used when. Looking at the ambiguities and redundancies in the system, Ken Able of the State University of New York at Albany made an interesting proposal in the late 1970s: he suggested that some species use several cues, and use them in a hierarchical fashion. If this is true, a bird capable of reading stellar, solar, magnetic, wind, and olfactory cues can switch from one to another depending on their availability and usefulness. On cloudy nights, for example, the stars are not visible, and sometimes magnetic storms or magnetic anomalies in the earth make magnetic cues unreliable. Then a migrant can resort to other cues. Able's synthesis has two important implications: that the avian navigational system is plastic, and that natural selection does not fine-tune the decision-making process of migrants. Instead, migrants are able to change their behavior to suit existing conditions and thus complete their migration in a timely, efficient, and safe manner.

How High Birds Fly

SPECTACULAR STORIES ABOUT BIRDS FLYING AT HIGH ALTITUDES abound. A vulture was once reported to have collided with a jet at 37,000 feet (11,300 meters) above the African plains, and hawks reportedly pass over Panama at more than 20,000 feet (6,000 meters). These examples, if true, make interesting reading, but they do not tell us how high birds *migrate.*

There is no simple answer to the question of how high birds migrate. Ten feet (3 meters), 1,000 feet (300 meters), 10,000 feet (3,000 meters): all are correct, at least for some birds, some of the time. You may have seen the low-altitude flight of loons, scoters, and pelicans, whose wings sometimes touch the waves, and then spotted some of the same species flying so high that they are barely visible through binoculars. These extremes within single species illustrate how variable the height of migratory flight can be and how birds change their behavior according to weather and topography and in special situations.

THE ALTITUDE OF POWERED MIGRANTS

In general, powered migrants are capable of flying at a greater range of altitudes than soaring migrants. Within minutes, birds using powered flight can climb or descend to whatever level of the atmosphere promotes the most efficient, safe, and rapid flight—anywhere from one foot to several thousand feet above the ground or water.

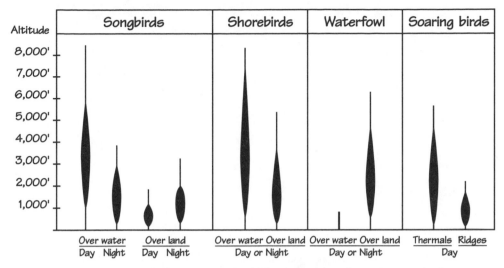

The altitudes at which migrating birds fly depend largely on how and where they are flying. Powered fliers prefer high altitudes, to avoid overheating; raptors generally don't fly over water.

Different kinds of powered migrants fly at different altitudes. Songbirds fly lower, on average, than most ducks and shorebirds. Study after study has confirmed that the bulk of nocturnal migration by songbirds occurs in the first 2,000 feet (600 meters) above the surface. Radar studies conducted in the eastern United States have shown that more than 75 percent of songbirds migrate within this stratum, and most other radar studies done over land agree.

Shorebirds and ducks may fly within this layer but frequently fly somewhat higher. A study in Switzerland, for example, revealed that larger radar echoes, presumably from shorebirds, were seen more often than songbird echoes in the atmospheric strata above 3,000 feet (900 meters). Similar results come from studies in North America.

The altitude of migrating waterfowl is probably the most variable of any group of birds. At times they fly at several thousand feet; at other times they fly just above the waves. The migratory flight of ducks and other waterbirds near shore is usually within 100 to 200 feet (30 to 60 meters) of the waves. In studies along the Atlantic coast, Cape May Bird Observatory researchers noted that more than

By flying close to the waves, the White Pelican uses ground effect—reduced drag from vortices formed as the wings move through the air.

90 percent of thousands of scoters, mergansers, black ducks, loons, gannets, and other birds flew at less than 200 feet (60 meters) above the waves. Scoters and loons can usually be seen within 20 to 30 feet (6 to 10 meters) of the water.

Why do some birds fly so close to the water? One explanation is *ground effect*. By flying within one wingspan of the surface, these birds may reduce the drag that occurs as a wing generates large vortices at the tip and along the trailing edge. This so-called induced drag increases the energy required for flight, but as a bird's wing tips come close to the waves, these vortices stick to the water's surface and are shed more easily. Low-altitude flight is also a means of avoiding headwinds or lateral winds. Near the surface of the waves or in the wave troughs, wind is not as strong as it is a few feet higher because of the friction, or drag, created by the water's surface. The result is a gradient of wind speed, with wind speed increasing with height above the surface. These explanations are educated speculation. By keeping low, a powered migrant flying over water makes better time at less cost.

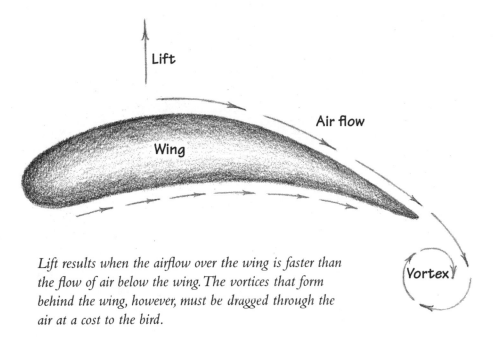

Lift results when the airflow over the wing is faster than the flow of air below the wing. The vortices that form behind the wing, however, must be dragged through the air at a cost to the bird.

THE ALTITUDE OF SOARING MIGRANTS

Hawks, pelicans, storks, swallows, gulls, and some other birds rely on soaring flight to varying degrees during migration. Soaring flight is much less costly than powered flight because the migrant uses not its own energy but rising air currents for lift. Soaring migration, then, can occur only when updrafts are abundant and powerful.

For soaring birds, a day of migration starts as the earth is heated by the sun's rays and thermals begin to form. In mid-September in eastern North America this occurs usually after 8 A.M. The first thermals are small and weak and thus difficult to ride, so soaring at this time of day is interspersed with powered flight. Species like Broad-winged and Sharp-shinned hawks can use thermals earlier in the day than larger species, like Red-tailed Hawks, Bald Eagles, and Ospreys, because they are able to soar in tighter circles and can also exploit weaker thermals because they do not sink as rapidly.

By midmorning thermals become stronger, larger, and more abundant. At this time most migrants can soar from 600 up to 1,500 feet (200 to 450 meters) or even higher. Progress is still slow,

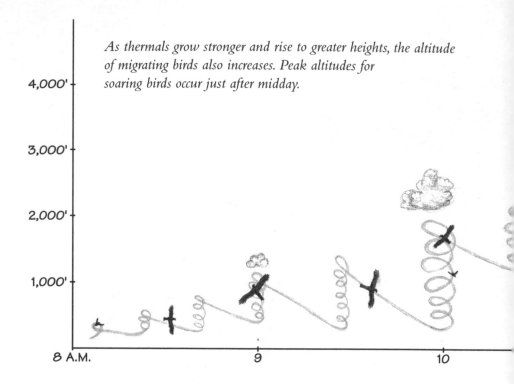

As thermals grow stronger and rise to greater heights, the altitude of migrating birds also increases. Peak altitudes for soaring birds occur just after midday.

however, because glides are short and usually at slow speeds. After midmorning and into midday, thermals are large and powerful. On the best soaring days thermals are so strong and so abundant that migrants can really begin to cover ground. By early to midafternoon thermals have reached their maximum, so this is when soaring migrants attain their highest altitude. In most of North America maximum altitude is usually less than 3,500 to 4,000 feet (1,100 to 1,200 meters) and only infrequently exceeds 5,000 feet (1,500 meters).

Soaring during midday is characterized by constant changes in altitude. Roughly half of a migrant's time is spent climbing and the other half gliding in the preferred migratory direction. The range of altitude used by migrants during gliding and thermal soaring is called the height band, the difference in altitude between the top and the bottom of a climb or glide. For migrating hawks the height band is greatest during midday to midafternoon, when it can be as great as 1,500 to 2,500 feet (450 to 750 meters). Radar studies show

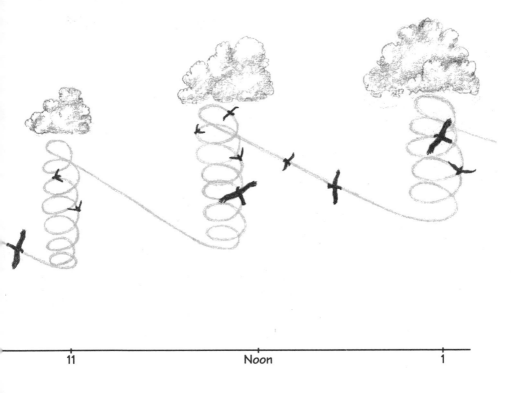

11   Noon   1

that the height band typically ranges from 700 to 1,600 feet (200 to 500 meters).

Climb rates in thermals vary greatly. Early in the morning, when thermals first form, updrafts at the core of a small thermal are weak, being only slightly greater than the sink rate of a soaring bird. The net gain in altitude is therefore small. At midday, thermals are large and strong, so vertical velocities of soaring birds at that time are three to five times greater than the sink rate, making conditions excellent for migration. The fastest a raptor can climb in a thermal is a little more than 10 miles (16 kilometers) per hour—straight up.

Hawk watchers frequently speculate on whether hawks soar into or above clouds. Radar studies have shown that flight in or above cumulus clouds is rare. Occasionally, eagles, Broad-winged Hawks, and other soaring birds enter the bottom of a cumulus cloud because lift at the cloud's base can be excellent. The birds seem reluctant to remain with the clouds, however, and most exit the cloud at the bottom or side shortly after entering. For soaring migrants it is safe to

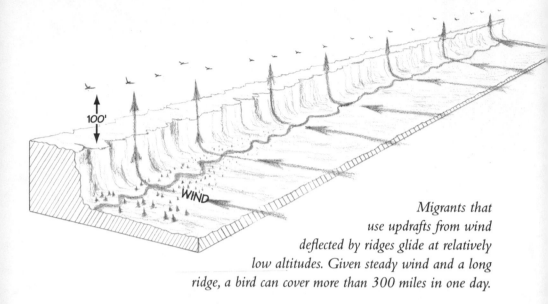

Migrants that
use updrafts from wind
deflected by ridges glide at relatively
low altitudes. Given steady wind and a long
ridge, a bird can cover more than 300 miles in one day.

say that flight in clouds is rare, and when it does occur, the birds seldom remain in the clouds for long.

Besides thermals, hawks also use updrafts created by wind deflected off trees or ridges. Altitude during ridge-gliding flight is usually lower than thermal soaring. Instead of changing altitude constantly, ridge-gliding Red-tailed Hawks maintain a nearly constant altitude for many miles. During this type of migratory flight, altitude can be as low as 5 to 20 feet (meters) or as high as 600 feet (200 meters) above the tree or ridge top. If the ridge is long and lift is constant along its length, migrants need not change altitude or soar in circles; they simply glide onward toward their destination while maintaining altitude. Ridge-gliding can be an efficient way to migrate provided the ridge is oriented in the right direction. The ability to change from thermal soaring to ridge-gliding shows how plastic the behavior of these birds really is—and indicates that they do make decisions.

Some soaring species, such as frigatebirds, gannets, pelicans, albatrosses, petrels, shearwaters, gulls, and terns, migrate over water. Although these birds are not completely dependent on soaring flight during migration, they do take advantage of updrafts to reduce the energy cost of flight. Many of these birds migrate for extremely long distances. Some shearwaters, for example, move more than 12,500 miles (20,000 kilometers) each year. By soaring and gliding, they greatly reduce the amount of energy required for migration.

The altitude of migration for most of these species has rarely been examined because it is difficult to study these birds when they are actually migrating. Many stay well off shore and are rarely seen during migration, so it is not surprising we know so little about their flight behavior. We do have some anecdotal information, however. The thermals that sometimes form over water in tropical or subtropical latitudes are weaker than those over land, rarely exceeding 4 miles per hour (2 meters per second) in vertical velocity or extending more than 1,000 to 2,500 feet (300 to 750 meters) above the ocean. These thermals are often marked by the shallow, nondistinct cumulus clouds common over tropical seas. They are neither strong nor abundant, but they do offer lift for those species adroit enough to take advantage of them. Frigatebirds soar to more than 1,000 feet (300 meters) above the ocean, and it seems that these and some other seabirds use these thermals to migrate.

Albatrosses, petrels, shearwaters, and other seabirds usually migrate within 30 to 100 feet (10 to 30 meters) of the water's surface and are rarely seen at altitudes exceeding 150 feet (45 meters). Their flight is characterized by long, sloping glides or powered glides near the surface, followed by short but steep ascents in wind updrafts off waves. This is not much different from a Sharp-shinned Hawk's gaining lift from wind deflected off trees or a ridge. The difference is that waves are not as large as ridges and are spaced more regularly, so the process can be repeated over and over.

A second mode of gaining altitude that may be used by some seabirds is by a process called dynamic soaring, which relies on the gradient in wind speed above the surface of the water. Scientists debate whether birds can use this gradient. Dynamic soaring requires a complex set of behaviors involving turning, reduction of speed, and downwind glides during which birds accelerate rapidly. I believe that seabirds can use dynamic soaring. Birds live in a very different sensory and "motor" world, which enables them to adjust their flight to changes in wind and updrafts we can hardly detect. Whether seabirds use wind deflected off the waves or dynamic soaring, most migrate at less than about 150 to 200 feet (45 to 60 meters).

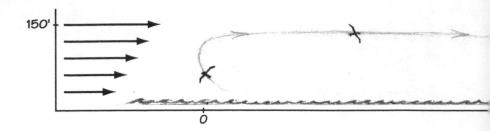

SELECTING A CRUISING ALTITUDE

Migrants of all sorts adjust their altitude to wind conditions. Because of drag created by the earth's rough surface, a gradient of wind speed occurs in the atmosphere: wind at higher altitudes is stronger than wind near the surface. Migrants capitalize on this gradient by flying higher with tailwinds and lower with headwinds. By doing this they are able to travel farther per unit of energy expended. It is, then, cost effective to vary altitude depending on wind direction and speed.

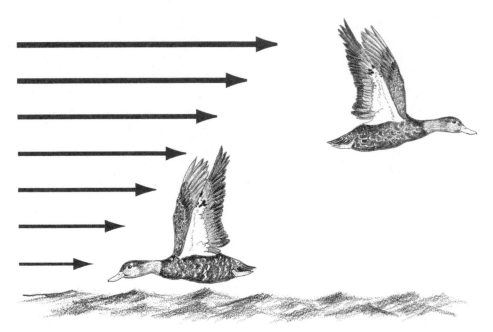

Powered fliers like Black Ducks also take advantage of wind gradients, flying lower into headwinds and higher with tailwinds to keep their energy costs low.

1,500'

Seabirds exploit wind gradients over the ocean. Turning abruptly into the wind, an albatross gains altitude, is lifted by the stronger winds well above the waves, and then turns downwind to ride a long glide. This dynamic soaring enables an albatross to cover great distances at low cost.

Some of the first researchers to document this phenomenon used a tracking radar in Switzerland to study the nocturnal migration of songbirds and some shorebirds. They also found that migrants selected nights and altitudes having favorable winds. Waterfowl, cormorants, shorebirds, and others also fly higher with tailwinds than with headwinds.

CASE STUDY	*Loons and Ducks Choose Low Altitudes along the Jersey Shore.*

WHILE STUDYING LOON AND DUCK MIGRATION ALONG THE NEW JERSEY shore in fall, my colleagues and I noted that Red-throated and Common loons, all three species of scoters, Red-breasted Mergansers, Oldsquaws, other sea ducks, and cormorants flew higher with tailwinds than with headwinds. When winds were opposing, these species flew within 5 to 7 feet (2 meters) of the waves, and they flew at 20 to more than 100 feet (6 to 30 meters) with following winds. By flying close to the waves, these birds avoid opposing winds. This is particularly the case when they fly in the troughs between the waves, where wind is virtually nil. It is amazing to watch these birds encounter a wave. They gain altitude only long enough to clear the wave, then descend to skim the water. At times, it is obvious that they prefer to fly very low. ■

There are, however, situations in which migrants' choice of altitude is very different from what occurs most often in most places. These special cases occur almost invariably when birds must fly over inhospitable habitat, as when songbirds must cross large expanses of water or when loons, grebes, and other waterfowl must pass over land. These are perilous situations. Songbirds cannot land on water and loons and grebes cannot take off from land—in either case, landing means death.

While studying spring songbird migration over the Gulf of Mexico in coastal Louisiana, Sidney Gauthreaux used weather radars in Lake Charles and New Orleans. He found that migrants arriving from the Yucatan at night flew mostly at or below 2,000 feet (600 meters)—about the same altitude that nocturnal migrants flew over land. But then, as the sun rose, the migrants climbed to higher altitudes, often double that of the birds flying before sunrise. These birds continued at high altitudes even after crossing the Gulf coast and often continued to migrate 60 or more miles (100 kilometers) inland even during daylight. He didn't need radar to track them: the flocks of Scarlet Tanagers, warblers, orioles, and other species could be seen flying in daylight through his 20-power spotting scope and binoculars.

This diurnal flight at high altitudes—not to mention in flocks— is unusual for nocturnal migrants. The term dawn ascent was coined by a British biologist to describe an identical behavior observed with radar among European Robins arriving in autumn in Great Britain from Scandinavia over the North Sea. Why do these migrants fly higher after sunrise? Plausible though not mutually exclusive answers include better visibility for sighting landmarks, more favorable winds aloft, and cooler air at higher altitude.

A corollary of the dawn ascent phenomenon is evident in the overland flight of loons, grebes, and some waterfowl, which these birds undertake at high altitudes. While studying hawk migration with radar in central New York, I found that Common Loons and some ducks regularly migrated 3,000 to more than 5,000 feet (900 to 1,500 meters) above the ground. At these altitudes they are difficult to see without binoculars. Over the nearshore waters of the Atlantic Ocean, they migrate only a few meters above the waves. Based on flight direction, these birds probably were flying nonstop between the eastern end of Lake Ontario and the Atlantic Ocean off New York and Connecticut. Scandinavian biologists have made similar observations of migrating eiders and Oldsquaws in Scandinavia. Using radar, they found that when over water, these birds flew at altitudes less than 300 feet (100 meters), but when crossing the Scandinavian peninsula, they flew at altitudes of 2,000 and 6,000 feet (600 and 800 meters). By flying at such high altitudes, these migrants probably benefit from cooler air, less atmospheric turbulence, stronger tailwinds, and long-distance visibility. Certainly the ability to sight water is especially important among birds that cannot take off from land.

Similarly, the long-distance overwater flight of some songbirds and shorebirds is done at very high altitudes. Semipalmated Sandpipers, Red Knots, Golden Plovers, and a few songbirds, including the Blackpoll Warbler, leave New England and the Canadian Maritime provinces during autumn and fly nonstop to the northern coast of South America. Their marathon flight is almost entirely over water. Radar observations show that birds fly over the coast of Nova Scotia at normal nighttime migration altitudes, but over Puerto Rico and some other locations these birds often travel at 5,000 feet (1,500 meters) and sometimes more than 12,000 feet (3,600 meters). These qualify as some of the highest known flights for migrants. At such high altitudes the birds can take advantage of tailwinds and cooler air temperatures, perhaps avoiding overheating and excess evaporative water loss.

The morning flight of songbirds is another special case. Nocturnal migrants that have landed before sunrise frequently undertake short morning flights after sunrise to select stopover habitat. At this time they do not fly as high as at night, nor do they fly as long. Birders in Cape May and elsewhere have witnessed this type of flight by warblers, vireos, tanagers, orioles, gnatcatchers, kinglets, and some sparrows. Morning flight at these sites is often at treetop level or only a few feet above the forest. Over unforested areas these birds fly higher. It is not known how high they climb, but studies of morning flight by researchers working in South Carolina, Minnesota, New York, New Jersey, and elsewhere reveal that most of this flight is below 600 feet (200 meters). About 90 percent of morning flights occur in the first two hours after sunrise.

CONSTRAINTS TO HIGH-ALTITUDE MIGRATION

For soaring migrants the primary constraint to high-altitude migration is atmospheric structure. These birds must fly in the convective layer of the atmosphere, where updrafts are abundant, strong, and predictable. Without thermals or mechanical updrafts, these migrants either do not fly or fly at low altitudes.

Powered migrants face different challenges. For them the most critical factor is the energy cost of climbing to very high altitudes. Because ascending to high altitudes is expensive, most migrants do not fly above 3,000 feet (900 meters). Only on very long flights is high-altitude migration efficient.

The scarcity of oxygen at high altitudes might also seem to be a constraint, because powered migrants need oxygen to metabolize fat. Consider the human mountaineer: because of the low partial pressure of atmospheric oxygen at high altitudes, humans must have supplemental oxygen or risk hypoxia (lack of oxygen) at more than about 10,000 feet (3,000 meters). This is not the case for birds, however, because their anatomy and physiology are different. Birds have air sacs that permit comfortable flight at altitudes of 18,000 to 20,000 feet (5,500 to 6,100 meters) above sea level. Vance Tucker, an avian physiologist, flew House Sparrows—a species that does not migrate—in a wind tunnel whose oxygen partial pressure was regulated to simulate high altitude. The House Sparrows were perfectly capable of flying at altitudes of over 18,000 feet (5,500 meters), demonstrating that most birds are physiologically capable of flying at much higher altitudes than they normally select for migration.

By this time you realize that the altitude at which birds migrate is extremely variable. Even after separating powered migrants from soaring migrants and comparing species, we still see a large amount of variation. Much of this variance can be attributed to weather, atmospheric structure, time of day, topography, and so forth. Birds are capable of making decisions and changing their behavior. This behavioral plasticity is adaptive, and without it birds could not migrate as quickly and as efficiently as they do.

TWELVE

Flocking Behavior during Migration

A GAGGLE OF GEESE, A KETTLE OF HAWKS, A BEVY OF QUAIL . . . I PREFER to call a group of birds a flock because the term implies social function or common purpose. Flocks are groups of birds that behave in a synchronous fashion, have cohesive movement, and maintain a relatively constant dispersion of individuals.

The most visible flocking behavior occurs among Canada Geese, Double-crested (and other) Cormorants, pelicans, Sandhill Cranes, and hawks. On cold November days it is not uncommon to see dozens or even hundreds of these birds flying in Vs or other formations. Why do these birds fly in formation? Why do some birds migrate in flocks whereas others fly alone? Why do flocks of some species assume one particular configuration rather than another?

We know with a fair degree of certainty which birds flock and which do not. What is more difficult to know is *why* birds flock during migration.

TYPES OF FLOCKS

If you saw a group of starlings flying by, how would you describe their configuration? Is "amorphous blob" adequate? Descriptions of flocking behavior are rare in ornithological literature, and there is no accepted terminology for various flock configurations.

Most flock formations can be categorized as lines, compound

Skein

Echelon

Scoters and other sea ducks fly in line formations.

lines, or clusters. Line formations are the simplest. Ducks such as scoters often form long lines, sometimes called skeins, within which individuals fly in columns, one bird directly behind another. Scoters also fly in echelons, as do other ducks, many geese, cormorants, egrets, ibis, pelicans, and cranes: in this case, each individual flies behind and slightly to the side of the bird in front of it.

The V- and J-shaped formations used by geese and some ducks, cranes, pelicans, and others are common variants of line formations. Other types of line formations include the inverted J and the inverted V, but they either are rarely used by migrants or are variants of columns or echelons. They may also be transitional between different configurations or may occur when individuals change places in a flock.

Line formations sometimes become more complex, forming branched Vs, Ws, or Us. These are seen among most of the species that fly in Vs or other species listed above that fly in lines. These formations are mostly variants of the simpler line configurations. Generally, line configurations characterize those species that use continuous flapping flight. Birds that use bounding flight, in contrast, would have difficulty maintaining an even spacing among individuals in lines; the constant changing of altitude and speed would disrupt a line formation. An exception might be the line formations of pelicans and cormorants, which incorporate short glides in their flight.

Cluster formations may be the most common type of flocking, and also the least structured when it comes to individual spacing within the flock. Clusters may be globular or extended. Globular clusters can be seen in large flocks of starlings, cowbirds, grackles, and blackbirds. This type of flock is three-dimensional; that is, birds are stacked above and below each other as well as flying next to each other on a single plane. When a hawk chases a flock of starlings, they form a ball, flying closely together.

A cluster, seen sometimes in pigeons, is wider than it is long, different from an extended cluster, which is longer than it is wide; both

Flocks of Canada and Snow geese
are compound line formations—Vs, Js, and Ws.

Globular cluster

*Crows flock in
globular clusters.*

are two-dimensional, with the birds spread out in a plane, but can
also be three-dimensional if the birds stack themselves vertically as
well. I have seen gulls flying low over the water in both wide and
extended clusters, presumably searching for schools of fish or other
food. Sometimes blackbirds form extended clusters when migrating
or flying to and from roosting areas.

Broad-winged Hawks, Swainson's Hawks, Turkey Vultures, and
Mississippi Kites migrate in two basic flock configurations. The first
is a vertically extended, swirling cluster—obvious when large flocks,
sometimes including more than a thousand individuals, soar in
a thermal. At this time the hawks fly in circles, forming a vertical
column as they climb hundreds of yards into the sky. Because they
are in a thermal, they take the approximate shape of the thermal
core, which resembles a column. The second type of flock configura-

Broad-winged Hawks and other soaring birds form tightly spiraling clusters as individuals seek the area of strongest lift within a thermal.

tion is the extended cluster. Birds are spaced across their flight path in an extended cluster, usually several times longer than wide. I have seen these extended clusters stretch for more than a mile across the Texas sky.

Those examples cover most of the types of flocks normally used by migrants, but actual configurations do not always fit neatly into the categories. The terms are merely constructs that help scientists, birders, and of course, writers describe migrating birds.

More important than using correct terminology is understanding the function of flocking. Birds use a particular flock configuration for a reason. When they change their flocking behavior, as when migrating blackbirds move from an extended cluster into a globular cluster at the sight of a raptor, the function of that configuration may be revealed. Such changes suggest that natural selection shapes several aspects of birds' flocking behavior—that birds make decisions.

BIRDS THAT FLOCK

Some species migrate in flocks, some migrate alone. Be aware, though, that the following generalizations do not always hold.

• Songbirds that migrate at night usually do not fly in flocks: warblers (Old and New World), vireos, catbirds, thrashers, thrushes (Old and New World), sparrows, tanagers, orioles, grosbeaks, buntings, gnatcatchers, flycatchers.

• Songbirds that migrate in daytime migrate in flocks more often than night-migrating songbirds: crows, jackdaws, finches, blackbirds, cowbirds, grackles, robins.

• Shorebirds that migrate day or night often fly in flocks.

• Egrets, ibis, and herons flying in daytime often fly in flocks. Those flying at night may be alone.

• Soaring birds often migrate in flocks: pelicans, cranes, some hawks, falcons, eagles, vultures, and kites. There are some very social raptors, particularly falcons, and some very asocial raptors. Some species hitchhike with flocks of obligate flockers.

• Waterfowl, whether they fly at night or during the day, usually migrate in flocks.

• Loons often fly in loose, poorly organized flocks along coastlines but assume greater flock integrity over land.

• Seabirds seem to migrate in flocks: gannets, gulls, terns, alcids, shearwaters, some petrels.

• Swallows and swifts almost always migrate in flocks.

Those generalizations do not fully describe flocking among migrants, but they will serve as rough guidelines.

Because birds are difficult to observe as they migrate at night, there are conflicting data and disagreements about the flocking tendencies of nocturnal migrants. Earlier students of bird migration suggested that songbirds migrating at night did so in well-defined flocks. More recently, George Lowery and Bob Newman of Louisiana State University reported seeing only seventy-five flocks (1 percent) among their seventy-five hundred observations of migrants (mostly songbirds) crossing the moon. Frank Bellrose of the University of Illinois used a single-engine airplane equipped with spotlights to look at migrants as they flew through the autumn night sky. (It must have been rather bizarre to cruise at more than 70 miles [112 kilometers] per hour through the darkened night sky, looking for migrants in the lights of an airplane.) He concluded that lone birds were more common when migration was light, but flocks predominated when migration was heavy. Flocks accounted for about half the sightings on nights of heavy migration.

Several other studies indicate that nocturnally migrating songbirds mostly fly alone. One study of the migratory takeoff behavior of songbirds from woodlands along the northern Gulf coast suggested that the birds took off alone. A ceilometer aligned horizontally (rather than vertically as is standard) was used to make direct observations of migrants as they took off—a foolproof method that yields reliable data.

| CASE STUDY | *Night-Migrating Songbirds Fly Alone.* |

EVIDENCE THAT SONGBIRDS DO NOT FORM FLOCKS AFTER TAKEOFF comes from ceilometer and radar studies. Viewing a narrow cone of the night sky with ceilometer and binoculars, one researcher observed several thousand migrants during both spring and autumn migration through central New York. Using the time between passing migrants, he calculated the distance between migrants in the night sky. From this he concluded that most of the songbirds he observed were not in flocks and that flocking rarely occurred. He also determined that the small amount of flocking he did see happened more often in spring on nights when large numbers of migrants were aloft. He concluded that flocking probably did not play a significant role in navigation. ■

Some songbirds migrate in flocks by day but singly at night. We know this because single radar echoes, which would indicate flocks of birds, are rare at night. Instead, radar screens show a diffuse pattern. Sidney Gauthreaux's wonderful radar studies of spring migration in Louisiana show a snowlike pattern at night over the Gulf and distinct spots on the radar screen during daytime. The migrants are the same species, but their behavior changes.

In southern Sweden a biologist found that small, insectivorous songbirds migrating early in autumn (August and early September) and late in spring (May and early June) did not give clear radar echoes, showing that these warblers, chats, and flycatchers also migrate singly. Other radar studies from Europe indicate that red-wings, song thrushes, robins, fieldfares, blackbirds, and some others also do not seem to form flocks during night migration.

Spring migration studies from the Swiss Alps revealed that echoes on tracking radars were "almost exclusively single birds during the night, while flocks prevailed in the daytime." Again, small songbirds were very numerous at night. Because their data were so good, the researchers were able to determine that the birds were at least 150 feet (45 meters) apart, more typically 480 to 960 feet (150 to 290 meters)—within range for the birds to hear each other vocalizing.

It is possible that songbirds fly in loose, widely spaced associations at night. The nocturnal vocalizations, or call-notes, of warblers, thrushes, and many others are easy to hear from the ground, hundreds of feet below. These call-notes are given more frequently on nights when visibility is poor. I have a hunch that it is also more common in the hour or two before dawn, when birds are beginning to end their night's migration, and when birds encounter barriers to migration, possibly because larger numbers of birds pile up at these barriers.

Songbirds that migrate during daytime fly in flocks more often than nocturnal migrants. The blackbirds—red-wings, grackles, starlings, and cowbirds—almost always migrate in flocks of several dozen to several thousands. These flocks can be snakelike processions, trailing over hundreds of yards or even a mile (hundreds of meters to more than kilometers) from front to back. Finches, robins, Blue Jays, crows, and many other diurnal migrants fly in rather loose flocks. Radar studies from Europe have shown that starlings exhibit flocking behavior in both night and day.

Researchers have reached no consensus about the extent of flocking among songbirds migrating at night. Flocking has been reported in nocturnally migrating songbirds, but the proportion of migrants flying in flocks varies among studies and locations. Certainly some migrants fly in flocks, but most go it alone.

HOW FLOCKS FORM

The manner in which flocks form varies greatly among species. The most social species, like geese, seem to be in flocks from takeoff to landing, maintaining flock integrity during their entire migratory flight. Flocks of loons seem to form en route, with flock size changing with time of day. Loons may join other loons to form flocks, but they seldom remain together for long distances.

I have read that the takeoff of Broad-winged Hawks from forests can be explosive, involving the simultaneous exodus of hundreds or even thousands of individuals. This is not what I observed during spring migration in southern Texas, however. At the end of a day's flight, large flocks of Broad-winged Hawks descended into the forest canopy. When thermals began to form the following morning, these birds began to take off by ones, twos, and threes. The small groups rapidly moved northward while climbing in small, weak thermals. As they slowly climbed to altitudes of a hundred or two hundred feet, they floated off to the north, carried by southerly winds.

Later in the day, flocks of Broad-winged and Swainson's hawks could be seen flying by at high altitudes. When climbing in thermals, these birds formed tight, swirling, vertical clusters. When gliding between thermals, they formed extended clusters similar to a line of dancers doing the conga. On radar, Sidney Gauthreaux and I measured many of these flocks and found them to be at least 3,000 feet (900 meters) long. On one occasion the flocks extended more than a mile (1.6 kilometers). At times the radar screen showed echoes that resembled a bead chain, with extended clusters between the beads of birds climbing in thermals.

Throughout a day's migration, Sharp-shinned Hawks, Cooper's Hawks, Ospreys, Swainson's Hawks, and some other species were seen hitchhiking with the larger flocks of Broad-winged Hawks. With the exception of Swainson's Hawks and Mississippi Kites, these hawks never formed large, single-species flocks. Instead, they opportunistically flew with the broad-wings, presumably taking advantage of the thermals that the Broad-winged Hawks had found.

The flocking phenomenon is ripe for further study. How flocks form and the behaviors of individuals during flock formation and during a day's flight might yield new insight into why migrants fly in flocks.

REASONS TO FLOCK

Explanations of why some birds migrate in flocks generally fall into five categories:

Aerodynamic efficiency

There have been several attempts to relate flock configuration to aerodynamic efficiency. Most have been mathematical, but a few researchers have tried to study flocking birds in flight. One German aerodynamicist used cinematography to determine the distance and positioning among the birds in flocks and concluded that there was a phase relationship between wing beats of neighboring geese. But an American scientist found no such relation among Canada Geese flying in V formation. It is virtually impossible to measure the aerodynamic forces of lift and drag on wings of birds during migration, so this hypothesis has never been truly tested. It is likely that some aerodynamic advantage accrues to waterfowl, cormorants, ibis, and some other large species that migrate in flocks with fixed distances and angles between individuals. The V formation of ducks and geese

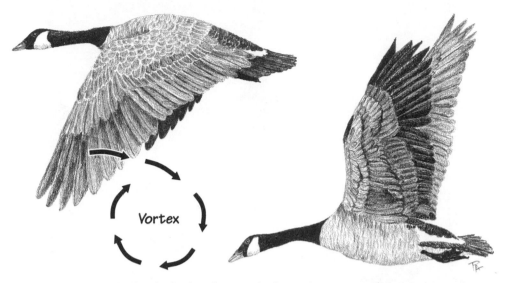

Canadas and other birds that fly in tight formations may realize aero-dynamic advantages if a bird can ride the wing-tip vortices created by the bird in front of it.

may represent the best possibility that there are aerodynamic advantages, at least to those individuals not leading the flock. Observations that birds take turns leading support this idea.

Line formations enable birds to follow closely head to tail or, in staggered lines as part of Vs, Us, or Ws. There may be an aerodynamic advantage from a reduction in the drag created by wing-tip vortices made by the bird ahead. Trailing birds may be able to flap in such a way that they use this vortex to their advantage, perhaps by reducing their own drag.

Finding thermals
The flocking behavior of soaring hawks at first seems incongruous. Indeed, predatory species usually spend much of their life alone. During migration, however, many raptors join others to fly in flocks. Aerodynamic advantage is not the reason: in most instances soaring birds that fly in flocks simply do not fly close enough to each other and their spacing varies too often for this to be the case. So why do raptors flock? Just as groups may be able to find food resources better

Flocking enables hawks to find thermals more easily. When one hawk is seen spiraling upward, other hawks flap their way to that thermal.

than individuals, soaring migrants that flock may be able to find and use thermals better than individual migrants.

Broad-winged and Swainson's hawks and Mississippi Kites, like other soaring migrants, divide their migratory time into gliding between thermals and climbing in updrafts. A rapid ascent in the strongest part of a thermal means that the bird can spend more time gliding toward its destination. To minimize the amount of time spent climbing in thermals, a migrant could assess the climb rates of other individuals to determine where the most powerful updrafts are. By avoiding birds that are climbing more slowly and flying toward birds that are climbing faster, individuals within the flock can reduce their soaring time. Similarly, by spreading out over, say, 60 to 300 feet (20 to 100 meters) during glides between thermals, soaring migrants may be able to locate thermals by random encounter. That is, by spacing themselves over a wide front during interthermal glides, birds can search a large area for thermals without deviating from their preferred migratory direction. When watching soaring migrants, I get the impression that this is what is happening. Videotaped flocks might yield information to confirm or refute this hypothesis.

Many hawks do not migrate with others of their own species, except in unusual circumstances. Instead, these birds are more often seen with groups of other hawk species. Why join other species? Again, perhaps to locate and use thermals more easily, by letting others sample the atmosphere.

Route finding

Because migration over long distances takes extraordinary navigation and orientation abilities, birds may be able to benefit from the experience of others. Among diurnal migrants that are long-lived, many individuals have completed the migration circuit at least once. These individuals may serve as leaders, teaching naive juveniles a migratory route. This would be especially true of migrants that have traditional pathways between breeding and wintering sites. Thus, migratory flight paths may be culturally transmitted from generation to generation.

Some researchers have suggested that by traveling in flocks, birds may reduce compass errors by averaging the orientational abilities of

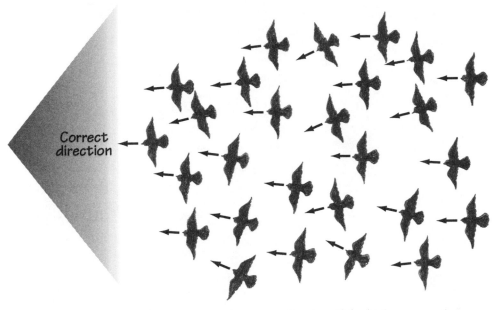

Flocking may help birds orient to the correct direction, if the birds average the directions taken by many individuals.

the many individuals in a flock. That is, the number of birds heading in the correct direction would compensate for the poor orientation of certain individuals. Testing this hypothesis is difficult, but Danish researchers studying the spring migration of Skylarks found that there was a relationship between flock size and the accuracy of orientation. Larger flocks oriented better, suggesting that flocking promotes better migratory orientation or navigation.

Detecting predators

Avoidance of predation is likely in only some species of birds that flock during migration. The idea that flocking is a means of predator avoidance is related to the many-eyes hypothesis: when several individuals are together, they need not spend as much time scanning for predators as when they are alone, thus gaining time to forage and, consequently, deposit more fat. Working against this theory is that only small, daytime migrants flying at very low altitudes are likely to be preyed on. Larger migrants—ducks, geese, gannets, large shore-

After a night of migration, warblers, vireos, tan-agers, and other songbirds form feeding flocks that help them find food and stay alert to predators, like Sharp-shinned Hawks.

birds, cranes, seabirds—flying during normal migration at several hundred to several thousand feet above the ground have few, if any, predators. Yet both large and small birds flock. I do not favor the predation hypothesis, except in rare circumstances.

Foraging

Another explanation of flocking that I don't favor is the foraging hypothesis. Following a line of reasoning like that for the predation hypothesis, the foraging theory is based upon the possibility that many birds will locate food more efficiently than lone birds. Among many species, flocking occurs mainly during migratory stopovers. Songbirds that fly alone at night quickly join other songbirds after dawn. These flocks are sometimes composed of one species but more often contain several. Individuals in these mixed-species flocks forage as they move through the vegetation. These flocks are not tight, cohesive units like flocks of waterfowl or shorebirds but instead are loose associations. Some glean insects off leaves, others probe bark crevasses for insects, some hawk flying insects from the air, and still others search for fruits. Flocks of ten to fifteen individuals of five to ten species of warblers are not uncommon in coastal areas of the East or Gulf coasts. Flocks of tanagers, vireos, and warblers are also common. It is possible that a migrating flock might be able to locate an isolated food source, especially if the birds migrate during daytime over open country.

CASE STUDY	*Warbler Flocks Forage in Atlantic Coastal Forests.*

THERE ARE NO TYPICAL FLOCKS OF WARBLERS. INSTEAD, THESE BIRDS form random aggregations. Flocks may include American Redstarts, Black-and-white Warblers, Northern Waterthrushes, Ovenbirds, Black-throated Blue Warblers, Red-eyed Vireos, Blue-gray Gnatcatchers, and many others. Black-and-white Warblers work the bark along the trunks and branches of trees, looking for insects. Redstarts hawk insects below the forest canopy or glean them off leaves. Black-throated blues work the upper canopy for fruit and insects.

The Red-eyed Vireo searches for insects on leaves or twigs above the middle canopy. Down below, Ovenbirds and waterthrushes are looking for insects in the leaf litter of the forest floor. The members of this mixed flock of songbirds possess different adaptations for feeding and feed on different types of foods. Nevertheless, these flocks retain some cohesiveness for many minutes or perhaps even hours, forming and re-forming, and always changing. Predator detection—the many-eyes hypothesis—seems to be the best explanation for these flocks. ■

It is obvious that because migrants are so varied in their flight behavior, no single explanation of why flocking occurs can be correct for all birds. Instead, we must examine flocking as a behavior shared by hundreds or thousands of species of birds. The function of flocking differs among species because of differences in selective forces that have shaped the evolution of social behavior in these animals. Among soaring migrants, flocking seems to be a means of locating and using lift more efficiently than lone migrants. Among songbirds, flocking occurs mostly among diurnal migrants that may be preyed upon. During migratory stopovers, these migrants probably form flocks to avoid predation and perhaps to find the best food resources. For some other species, orientation, navigation, or aerodynamic advantages may explain why these birds migrate in flocks.

THIRTEEN

The Calls of Migrating Birds

BIRDS ARE MARVELOUS SONGSTERS. THEIR SONGS AND CALLS ARE A delight—and so diverse that they are devilishly difficult for us to learn. With the appearance of dozens of commercial tapes, thousands of birders are rapidly learning to identify the songs of hundreds of species of North American and European birds. Another challenge exists, however, that is only now being discovered: that of learning call-notes, or chip-notes.

Call-notes are distinguished from song by their brevity and the context in which they are used. For the most part, birds sing during the breeding season either to advertise a male's territory or to attract a mate. Call-notes, on the other hand, are used year-round to keep in touch with other birds within a flock or convey warnings about predators. An example of a species with both a song and a call-note is the White-throated Sparrow. Its song is a whistled "Pooor Sam Peabody, Peabody, Peabody," with the "Sam Peabody" being about a musical fourth higher than the "Pooor." This song can be heard during late winter or early spring before the bird arrives at the breeding site, but it is usually not complete or is barely recognizable; then, in spring, it sings the real song. The call-note of the White-throated Sparrow, on the other hand, is a staccato "chink" or "tseeet." Some species do not possess what is called song, but do use distinct call-notes. For example, the Least Sandpiper has no real song but gives a shrill, hoarse "creeeennk" call mostly when in flight.

Thousands of birders are now diligently attempting to learn to identify the call-notes of birds. After all, plumage cannot always be observed, and true songs are heard only during breeding season. With the increased awareness of call-notes, some birders can help track migrating birds. Birds make call-notes during migration that are similar, or sometimes identical, to the call-notes they give at other times. Birders who learn to identify call-notes will be able to identify many species as they pass overhead at night or during the daytime.

Bill Evans, working in central New York, has taped thousands of nocturnal migrants of many species, but identifying the species of the callers is very difficult. In time, he will identify many more species. The best tape now available that is specifically for North American migrants was made by Evans. The tape is a no-frills recording of the different call-notes of North American thrushes. Unfortunately, Evans's tape of migrating Catharus thrushes is the only tape devoted entirely to call-notes by migrants, it deals with only a few species, and it is available at few stores.

Sounds of Migrating and Wintering Birds, a two-tape set produced in France, includes call-notes of many European migrants and, like Evans's tape, is published privately. The Cornell Laboratory of Ornithology's Library of Natural Sounds recommends these tapes for people birding in Europe, but to my knowledge they are not available in North America.

Many of the commercial tapes of bird song include some regular call-notes of species like Barn Owls and shorebirds, which can be used to identify migrants by sound. Many of the recordings on these tapes come from the Cornell Laboratory of Ornithology's Library of Natural Sounds. Researchers at this institution are diligently attempting to curate the sounds recorded by interested amateurs and professionals. In the near future more and better tapes will become available.

The vocalizations used by migrants seem to be variants of day-time call-notes. The calls are sometimes distinctive, but a trained ear is necessary to identify them. These vocalizations include a buzzy "beeeo" from a Veery, a harsh "wok" by a Black-crowned Night Heron, a "skwonk" by a Great Blue Heron, a high-pitched "szeeet" by warblers, a rapidly whistled "too-too-too" by a Greater Yellowlegs, a rusty "creeeenk" (the *r* being rolled quickly) by a Least Sandpiper, and a screeching "psheeeet" (accent at the end, with the end rising slightly up the scale) by a Barn Owl.

A problem with identifying calls of migrants that are flying at hundreds of feet above the earth in the darkness of night is that there are several sources of distortion. High-frequency calls attenuate with distance, and some of the frequencies cannot be heard. In addition, Doppler shifts distort the call-notes. These distortions make it virtually impossible to distinguish some species, such as the *Dendroica* warblers. And the calls themselves may be different at night, and at various times of night.

KEEPING IN TOUCH

Why would a Ruby-crowned Kinglet flying at more than 1,000 feet (300 meters) above the forests of New England make a sound? We don't know their precise function, but it is certain that these call-notes are given in a social context. A call-note given in the absence of other birds is wasted, so it is likely that migrants vocalize to stay in contact with one another. This raises two other questions. Do birds vocalize in response to other migrants' calls? Do migrants stay in contact during migration? Scientists have not yet studied these issues. The finding by Swiss biologists that migrating songbirds space themselves 150 to more than 600 feet (45 to 200 meters) apart demonstrates that many birds migrate within hearing range of other birds. Similar studies also suggest that on most nights, migrants are numerous enough that they are within earshot of each other. Perhaps when large numbers of birds are aloft or visibility is poor, vocalizations prevent midair crashes.

The nightly incidence of calling varies greatly. On some nights and in some places calls are incessant, and on others they can be heard only occasionally. One study showed little relationship between the number of calls heard at a given site and the number of birds migrating over that site. It seems that migrants call more often when visibility is poor, as in fog, or when they are disoriented. If the latter is correct, it implies some sort of social function for flocking.

More calls also seem to be heard at sites where birds are confronted with a barrier to migration. Nocturnally migrating birds seem to call more often along coastlines, for example, than inland. In Cape May, where extraordinary numbers of songbirds congregate, more calls are heard within a few hundred feet of the Atlantic Ocean than at sites half a mile (one kilometer) or so inland. Whether there are more migrants close to the coast or whether they simply call more is not known. Though these nocturnal migrants do not fly in tight, cohesive flocks, they may maintain some sort of communication with one another.

Once migrants have landed, the incidence of calling also can be great, especially in the postdawn period when migrants are active. At this time call-notes certainly have a social function: they facilitate the formation of flocks. Call-notes may also allow members of a flock to stay in loose association while foraging or moving through or between habitats. Members of a loosely spaced flock can thus still realize the advantages of flocking. Presumably, natural selection has shaped this behavior.

To hear migrants during the migration season, go to a quiet place. Or join a group. Patricia Sutton of the Cape May Bird Observatory leads night programs in the fall to listen and watch for migrating owls and other birds. The program is a combination of watching for birds in the beam of the lighthouse and listening for the migrants as they fly overhead. On a calm night participants will hear thrushes, warblers, herons, egrets, shorebirds, and even a Barn Owl or two. Another example is the Lunar Lunacy program given by Mike Anderson at New Jersey Audubon Society's Scherman-Hoffman Sanctuary. Other nature centers have similar programs, which are becoming more popular every year. Not only do they teach people about migrants and other animals that make noises in the night, but they are also lots of fun. Each autumn people come away satisfied with having "observed" migrants with their ears. Listening to migrants pass overhead is a restful and enjoyable way to pass an evening. And between migrant call-notes, you can take in the stars, crickets, frogs, and other night sounds.

FOURTEEN

Flight Strategies

MIGRATORY FLIGHT IS A RESULT OF MANY DECISIONS. TO COMPLETE migration successfully, birds must make thousands of decisions and they must make them correctly. Errors delay migration or even lead to death. Throughout this book I have emphasized that birds make decisions, most often about a single behavior. Birds decide, for example, what time of day to fly, at what speed to fly, how high to fly, in which direction to fly, and where to land.

We have seen that some decisions are "hard-wired," determined by messages encoded in a bird's genetic makeup. These behaviors do not vary and cannot be modified by the environment—at least not in the short term. Some first-time migrants, for example, are genetically programmed to fly a fixed distance or time in a predetermined direction, then change direction. The directional behavior of these birds is not learned but innate.

Other decisions are contextually dependent: the bird's behavior changes according to the situation. Decisions based on past experience are learned behaviors, like the final stages of a migrant's journey to a wintering or breeding site with which it has previous experience. The migrant is familiar with the topography and may have learned how to locate the specific place based on known landmarks.

Most decisions are a blend of genetically determined and learned aspects of behavior, but the mix has puzzled scientists. Animal behaviorists now maintain that animals are genetically programmed to learn. The ability to learn is, in itself, one of the most important of adaptations.

Together, the set of decisions made by a migrant constitutes a strategy. It is not necessary to assume that birds make conscious decisions or that they have the ability to reason. Similarly, we need not resort to anthropomorphic arguments when we discuss decision making and strategies. In natural history, scientists study reproductive strategies, territorial strategies, foraging strategies, and several other strategies. The term *strategy* has been the jargon of evolutionary biologists for decades, whether the scientist studies physiology, behavior, ecology, or anatomy. Migration partakes of all these disciplines. Tom Alerstam calls a strategy "a harmonious mixture of rigid and flexible behavior adapted to a bewildering number of factors affecting the safety and economics of the migratory journey." By *rigid,* Alerstam means a genetically programmed, relatively unchangeable, or fixed behavior. Natural selection, he says, acts "to maintain and refine the level of adaptation in the bird's journey." Again, as with the use of the term *decision,* I am not implying that a strategy reflects any *conscious* activity by migrants.

In modern ecology theorists and researchers who hold to the optimality theory believe that natural selection works in a way that optimizes the behavior of animals. In migration, one of the best examples of optimality is the selection of flight speed. Migrants fly at speeds that are not too fast and not too slow. The speeds are just right, permitting the birds to fly the greatest distance for the amount of energy used. This is only one behavioral aspect of migration, however.

If the decisions of migrants and their resultant strategies are products of natural selection, what does selection act upon? Does it operate on a single aspect of migration or on many together? And does natural selection operate more strongly on one behavior than on another? The answers to these questions are the firmament of migration study, but because scientists have never examined this elusive aspect of migratory behavior, we simply do not know enough about migration to determine how natural selection operates.

The question of how behavioral decisions are integrated into a migration strategy has been sadly neglected. Only a few researchers have examined two or three aspects of migration simultaneously. Tom Alerstam studied the speed and altitude of migrating Arctic Terns and found that they changed their airspeed with altitude. Ken

Able has examined flight direction as it relates to wind and flight speed, as has Bruno Bruderer. Their studies are among the rare attempts to determine how two aspects of migratory behavior are integrated and how the migrants' decisions about them relate to each other.

Sophisticated radar has enabled those researchers, and many others, to track the behavior of individual birds. Although radar will continue to be an important tool, I believe that the future of migration research is in the use of radiotransmitters. We have information about migrants' speed, altitude, daily timing, and flight direction, but we don't know how they make sequential, simultaneous sets of decisions. To gather the necessary data, we must follow individual migrants for most or, if we can, all of their journey. The radiotelemetry work of Alan Harmata with Bald Eagles in the Rocky Mountains and Great Plains of western North America shows that birds can be tracked through an entire migration. With enough funding, better technology, perseverance, and a great deal of luck, researchers will be able to track migrants from breeding to wintering grounds and back. During these studies, we will learn more about the decisions birds make and, consequently, how they make those decisions.

Consider a ½-ounce (15-gram) Prothonotary Warbler that breeds in, say, Ohio. In August it initiates migration and in September or October arrives at its Neotropical wintering site in Central America. The following April, this migrant will return to its Ohio breeding site in a tree-hole cavity, after flying nonstop over the Gulf of Mexico and then over the forests of the southeastern United States. By affixing a tiny radiotransmitter to the warbler's back and monitoring it by satellite and from the ground, we will be able to get geographic "fixes" on it every hour or two for many months.

The information gathered every ninety minutes or so will permit researchers to follow every move the bird makes. We will know whether and when it takes off every day, the weather at that time, how long it stops over, whether it makes false migrations prior to real flights, and hundreds of other important things about its migration. Because we will know its exact location, we can capture it to determine its body weight. We will even be able to observe moment-to-moment changes in altitude, direction, speed, and flocking behavior. And then we can learn how these aspects come together in a cohesive strategy for migration—one that ensures the successful completion of the migratory journey. Unfortunately, this type of miniaturization technology is not yet available, although smaller transmitters exist to follow these birds for short distances.

Another important part of this process is developing analytical tools to examine multiple sets of decisions. Psychologists and economists have developed mathematical and logical models that permit researchers to make predictions about several behaviors, but these models have yet to be integrated into migration research. Tom Alerstam has integrated optimality theory into his research, and this may be the solution, or at least part of it. Another solution may be a technique developed by psychologists who study how people make sets of decisions. This highly complex model, called parallel distributed processing, is now used to study how humans make decisions. The issue of how animals arrive at the decisions they make during migration is the true challenge for future research.

Migrants are extremely plastic, incredibly adaptable and able to change their behavior to suit the immediate needs of migration. Recall Alerstam's statement that migrants are adapted to a bewildering array of factors. If a migrant were not capable of changing its behavior—that is, making decisions based on weather, its fat condition, its proximity to the destination, and other factors—it could not migrate. There are simply too many things that are constantly changing in a bird's migratory world for its behavior to be genetically fixed. That is why a strategy with contingencies to meet changing environmental and other conditions must exist—and why studying this aspect of migration is so important.

Fifteen

Conservation of Migrating Birds

THAT POPULATIONS OF BIRDS THROUGHOUT THE WORLD ARE DECLINING is well known. Ask the old-timers who have been birding for thirty years or more. Conservationists and wildlife managers are now becoming aware that the declines have been occurring for more than a century, with some species declining rapidly and others more slowly. The declines are widespread among songbirds, shorebirds, hawks, waders, waterfowl, loons, seabirds, and many others. Some species have even become extinct.

Today the decline of Neotropical migrants is of great concern to those of us who love and study birds. The blame was first placed on the destruction of the Central and South American forests where many birds wintered. As we learned more about these species, we began to realize that forest fragmentation in some parts of North America was also to blame because it shrinks breeding habitat and hurts breeding success in the remaining habitats. Most attention has thus focused on the breeding and wintering seasons, when individual birds occupy single, relatively small locations.

A few biologists, however, considered the possibility that songbirds and other migrants were vulnerable during their migrations as well. For some species, many birds die during their first migration. This and other mortality statistics have helped us realize that the health of populations of many migrants depends in large part on what happens during migration. Specifically, two types of human activity affect migrating birds: outright killing or disturbing migrants, whether deliberate or inadvertent, and alteration and destruction of the stopover habitats.

KILLING OF MIGRANTS

Migrating birds have been slaughtered for food and fun for millennia. The superabundance of migrants at some locations was seen as a blessing to indigenous peoples, who harvested migrating birds and stockpiled their meat for leaner times. One of the most vivid accounts of this harvest, probably not too far from factual, is given by James Fenimore Cooper in *The Pioneers,* set in the 1740s. Cooper describes a scene in which a mass migration of Passenger Pigeons is fired upon by villagers in upstate New York. Guns of all sorts, including a punt gun (a small cannon), were used to down thousands from among the vast flocks. According to Cooper, the millions of pigeons that passed had the effect of "shadowing the field like a cloud." Many of the birds that were shot in his story were left to rot. By the 1870s, migrant flocks of as few as twenty birds were deemed noteworthy in upstate New York. The species is now extinct.

A more recent equivalent of this slaughter occurred during the 1920s and 1930s at such famous hawk migration sites as Hawk Mountain and Cape May. Maurice Broun, the godfather of modern hawk watching, described the carnage along the ridges of Pennsylvania during autumn. The hundreds of thousands of hawks that passed at low altitudes were easy prey for gunners. In 1935 Roger Tory Peterson observed the shooting at Cape May and counted the raptors as they migrated past the gunners. In one of his books he even describes eating Sharp-shinned Hawk at a guest house in Cape May. For a family of four, one menu recommended twenty Sharp-shinned Hawks. (Owners of modern-day Cape May restaurants also love the hawks, not for food but for the millions of dollars spent by the birding tourists.)

The Eskimo Curlew, Red Knot, Golden Plover, and many other shorebirds were also coveted by market hunters in years past. Gunners shot hundreds of thousands, loaded their carcasses into barrels or

A typical year

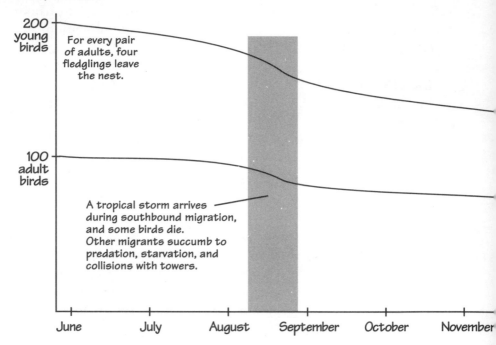

200 young birds

For every pair of adults, four fledglings leave the nest.

100 adult birds

A tropical storm arrives during southbound migration, and some birds die. Other migrants succumb to predation, starvation, and collisions with towers.

June   July   August   September   October   November

A year of severe weather

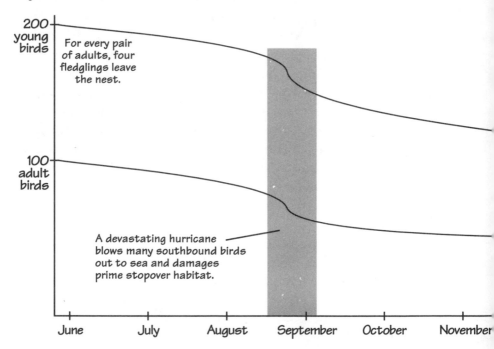

200 young birds

For every pair of adults, four fledglings leave the nest.

100 adult birds

A devastating hurricane blows many southbound birds out to sea and damages prime stopover habitat.

June   July   August   September   October   November

In a normal year, the number of birds in a species can remain stable despite mortality during migration. But in a year of severe weather, the population can crash; it will take several breeding seasons of mild weather before the population recovers.

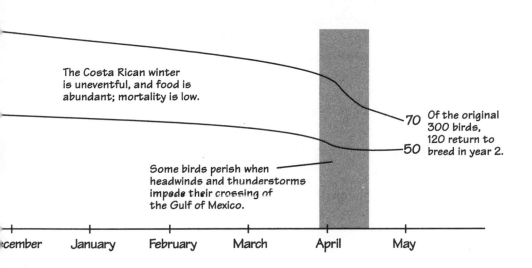

The Costa Rican winter is uneventful, and food is abundant; mortality is low.

70 Of the original 300 birds, 120 return to 50 breed in year 2.

Some birds perish when headwinds and thunderstorms impede their crossing of the Gulf of Mexico.

:cember   January   February   March   April   May

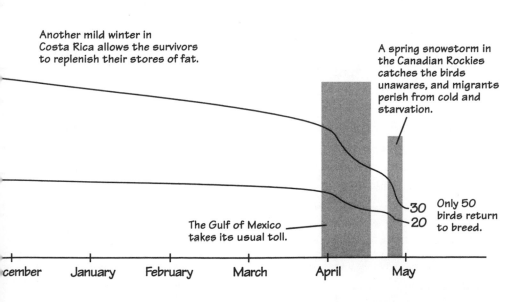

Another mild winter in Costa Rica allows the survivors to replenish their stores of fat.

A spring snowstorm in the Canadian Rockies catches the birds unawares, and migrants perish from cold and starvation.

The Gulf of Mexico takes its usual toll.

30 Only 50 birds return 20 to breed.

:cember   January   February   March   April   May boxcars, and shipped them off to the cities, where they were bought by people who never suspected that these birds could be exterminated. But they were: of the three species listed above, one may be extinct and the other two were greatly reduced.

The shooting has not been limited to North America. Yossi Leshem, director of the Society for the Protection of Nature in Israel, interviewed several hawk shooters in Lebanon. Some of them were more than sixty years old and had been shooting hawks for half a century. He concluded that a few shooters were capable of doing grievous damage. One old-timer had dispatched more than ten thousand hawks during his lifetime. Cranes, storks, and other large migrants are also shot in large numbers in this area. This type of shooting goes on in many places in the Middle East, where millions of soaring birds pass each autumn and spring. For the birds, it is like running a gauntlet several hundred miles in length.

A similar situation exists in southern Europe, particularly in southern Italy. While counting migrating hawks in southern Calabria, a research team heard more than five thousand reports from firearms during a single migration. Most of the shooting was directed toward the Honey Buzzards that were crossing from Sicily to Calabria as part of their trans-Mediterranean spring migration, although Peregrines, Ospreys, and others are also shot. Migrating hawks are shot regularly in several places in Sicily, Calabria, Malta, and probably North Africa. In Malta especially, stuffed raptors are highly desired as household ornaments.

Conservationists' efforts have resulted in the abolition of hawk shooting at most of the sites in North America. Hawk Mountain Sanctuary Association in Pennsylvania has been a leader in the effort to ban shooting of raptors in North America. People like Maurice Broun patrolled the ridge and stopped the shooting, at least on the sanctuary property. Many of the sons and daughters of those who shot hawks on the ridges of Pennsylvania are now staunch supporters of Hawk Mountain Sanctuary Association's efforts to protect hawks and other wildlife. It is important to note that *regulated* hunting for game species has never resulted in extinction. Licensed hunters in no way jeopardize populations of North American birds. Hunters, in fact, have saved more habitat that nonhunters, and without them we would not have a wildlife refuge system in the United States.

Efforts to stop hawk shooting in Sicily and Calabria in southern Italy have not been as successful as at Hawk Mountain. In recent years those opposing the practice have been beaten and shot at; a car-bombing even occurred in front of a Palermo hotel that hosted an anti–hawk shooting conference. Though there are laws that protect these and other birds in much of the world, in some places there is little enforcement.

Shooting is not the only method used to take migrants. Around the Mediterranean migrating songbirds are captured live. Because some areas of southern Europe have been stripped of trees, migrants are attracted to the few that remain. By coating small trees with sticky lime, or birdlime, bird harvesters can capture dozens, even hundreds, of migrants in a day. An older gentleman once informed me that he and his relatives caught birds this way while he was growing up in southern Italy; they captured and ate all kinds, he said. Some were sold in the marketplace.

In some parts of South America, people catch sandpipers and other shorebirds by stretching monofilament fishing line a few feet above tidal flats. When the birds arrive, flying fast and low, they collide with the nearly invisible fishing line and usually break a wing or neck. They are then collected and eaten.

Perhaps the most unusual method of catching wild birds involves grabbing them with bare hands. Inhabitants of the small islands between Japan and the Philippines used to make blinds in the tops of trees, from which they grabbed migrating hawks as they landed. The Gray-faced Buzzard Eagle (actually a kite) flies from China and Japan through the chain of islands called the Ryukyus on its way to wintering quarters in the Philippines. Exhausted from a long flight over water, the birds would alight in the first trees they saw. Islanders would grab them by their legs and pull them into the blind, and await the next migrants. The birds were used for food and as pets until the Japanese outlawed the practice. (Banders capitalized on this method and were able to band more than a thousand birds in only one or two seasons. They were able to determine that most of these birds fly to the Philippines because they had a 10 percent band recovery from birds shot there.)

These methods are but a few of those used throughout the world. Some migrants are taken for food, some as pets, and others for resale as pets or food. The taking of birds is illegal in many areas, such as Mexico, but that does not stop the killing. In much of Mexico one can purchase stuffed hawks and caged birds in the open marketplace.

INADVERTENT KILLING

Although many migrants are killed deliberately, others are killed inadvertently by changes in the landscape wrought by man. Migrating birds frequently collide with large buildings, towers, lights, guy wires, and windows. In fact, some of our best information about bird migration comes from tower kills. Thousands of birds are killed in collisions with radio and television towers each migration season in North America. By studying tower kills, we can learn which species of birds pass through a particular area and gather information about their seasonal passage. Tower kills, for example, have shown that large numbers of migrants fly only several hundred feet above the ground—information difficult to gather by standard research methods.

Few people realize the devastating effect the automobile has on migrating birds, since we usually picture migrants flying at hundreds or thousands of feet above the ground. But when the birds descend to look for habitats to rest and feed, they become vulnerable. Several papers report significant mortality of migrants that is attributable to automobiles. A three-year study from Spain reported more than four hundred Little Owls killed by automobiles, mostly during the postnesting dispersal period. A study I coauthored with M. Ross Lein of the University of Calgary focused on the mortality of Snowy Owls wintering and migrating in Alberta. We found that of seventy-one specimens for which a cause of mortality could be determined, ten were killed by cars and another forty-seven by collisions with unknown objects, including automobiles, fences, and power or telephone lines.

CASE STUDY	*Tree Swallows and Saw-whet Owls Are Struck on the Garden State Parkway.*

NATURAL HISTORY WRITER PETE DUNNE HAS CALLED THE AUTOMOBILE "New Jersey's top predator." He couldn't have said it better. One blustery October morning I saw Tree Swallows fly down to the warm pavement of the Garden State Parkway to rest or bask in the sun. Cars struck them; as the injured birds on the asphalt attempted to fly, more swallows landed. It took only a few minutes for more than four hundred migrants to die. To end the carnage, several of us dodged oncoming cars as we kicked the bodies of the birds off the road. Once the birds were off the pavement, no others tried to land. More often, a single bird will be hit while trying to cross or forage on or beside a road. An avid naturalist named George Loos collected owls and hawks along a 40-mile segment of the parkway—he did not count the thousands of dead catbirds, robins, rails, warblers, woodcocks, and other species that are regularly seen along this road. His total from one decade was more than 250 hawks (four species) and owls (four species), with more than 100 being the tiny, three-ounce Saw-whet Owl. The large number of these birds and seasonal timing of his finds showed that this species was more common than believed during winter in South Jersey winter and migration. The increase in traffic and number of roads will definitely affect owl populations. ■

Although collisions with towers and automobiles are two common causes of nonnatural mortality among migrants, windows are perhaps the biggest killers. Recent work has documented that millions of birds die annually after colliding with windows. It is likely that a substantial proportion of these are migrants.

DISTURBANCE OF FORAGING OR RESTING BIRDS

A bird need not be shot or trapped for it to be removed from the breeding population. Depriving a bird of time to rest and forage has the same result as killing it outright: if it does not feed and deposit fat, it will not complete migration successfully and will not breed.

Disturbance from humans can be as simple as cars passing an area or a person walking on a beach. A Peregrine Falcon or a Bald Eagle may not tolerate a human nearby when it is hunting or resting. A shorebird may not forage when it detects a human beachcomber. Warblers cannot eat in a yard while being stalked by a cat or a dog.

| CASE STUDY | *Education Protects Northbound Shorebirds Feeding on Horseshoe Crab Eggs.* |

ALONG THE DELAWARE BAYSHORE, WHERE A MILLION SHOREBIRDS STOP over during spring migration to feed on horseshoe crab eggs before continuing to the tundra, human disturbance is a major problem. The beaches used by the Red Knots, Ruddy Turnstones, Sanderlings, and Semipalmated Sandpipers are also popular with humans. As the birds feed, they are harassed almost constantly by beachwalkers, dogs, ultra-light planes, fishermen, photographers, off-road vehicles, and even birders. When disturbed, they must take flight, circle, land, and begin feeding again. On weekends some prime beaches are subject to so much disturbance that the birds do not even use them, despite the superabundance of horseshoe crab eggs. The problem is so bad that the New Jersey Endangered and Nongame Species Program and the Cape May Bird Observatory have joined together to get students from nearby Stockton State College to patrol the beaches on weekends during the migration season. Their responsibility is to educate beachgoers about the needs of the knots and turnstones. By talking to people about the birds and their migrations, these teacher-wardens have made many people more sensitive to the birds' needs. Education works! ■

Birds inhabiting open habitats such as marshes, beaches, and fields are more susceptible to disturbance than forest birds, which are generally more tolerant of humans as long as there are places to flee. As habitats grow smaller, however, there are fewer places for birds to take refuge, and human pressure takes its toll.

HABITAT DESTRUCTION AND ALTERATION
Habitat destruction is analogous to a game of musical chairs: everyone must find a seat when the music stops, but when one seat is

removed, there are not enough seats for everyone, and one person is left standing. This analogy was first made by Pete Dunne to describe what is happening to birds as they migrate through New Jersey. As most of the habitat along the coast is converted into housing and other development, there are fewer and fewer sites where birds can rest and forage during migration. Without such sites, some birds will not complete their migration, and their genes will be lost to future generations.

All birds that migrate need habitat: shorebirds need beaches, mudflats, grassy meadows, and streamsides; songbirds need woodlands, brushy areas, marshes, and grassland; hawks and owls need forests, meadows, marshes, brushland, and grassland; ducks need open water, marshes, rivers, streams, and mudflats.

When a bird stops migrating, it must find a safe place to rest, forage, and in some cases drink water. A Yellow-rumped Warbler, for example, must stop where there is an abundance of fruits and insects to eat near thick brush or woods where it can take refuge from a Merlin or Sharp-shinned Hawk that is also making a migratory stopover. If it finds food but no cover, it may put on migratory fat only to be preyed upon while doing so.

A warbler in your backyard may not be able to meet its needs. It may be a target for your cat, or it may not have found food. If you observe that same warbler several hours later, chances are it has found most of the things it requires. If it hadn't, it would have moved on.

CASE STUDY	*City Destroys Migrants' Habitat.*

ONE OF THE MOST THOUGHTLESS RAZINGS OF MIGRATORY BIRD HABITAT was done by the city of North Wildwood, New Jersey, in 1989, when it cut an 18-acre (7-hectare) dune forest. The area was even sprayed with a chemical to inhibit fruiting. This forest of bayberry bushes, which grew to nearly 13 feet (4 meters), supported an abundance of migrating birds, including thousands of Tree Swallows and Yellow-rumped Warblers, which ate the berries, and Merlins and Sharp-shinned Hawks, which in turn ate the swallows and warblers. Why were the bayberries cut? Motel owners complained that their clients couldn't see the ocean from their swimming pools. Moreover, the Tree Swallows frequented the motel swimming pools, drinking from them and leaving droppings. That same year this municipality received some $100,000 of taxpayers' money from the federal government for dune restoration and protection. The cost of cutting the bayberries was about $35,000. What is more incomprehensible is that the state Department of Environmental Protection's Division of Coastal Resources allowed an action that was injurious to both the dune system and migratory birds. ■

Bird biologists have learned which habitats are used by breeding birds through the use of sophisticated statistical analysis and enormous data sets. We also know quite a bit about the needs of birds during the nonbreeding season. Until recently, biologists had not studied the habitat needs of migrants; now we are trying furiously to fill this gap in our knowledge.

The Nature Conservancy recognized in the early 1980s that habitat destruction along migration pathways of some species was a significant problem. The group responded by purchasing several important tracts in Cape May that were used by large numbers of migrating hawks, shorebirds, and songbirds.

More recently, the Nature Conservancy, in collaboration with the Cape May Bird Observatory and wildlife agencies in New Jersey, Virginia, Delaware, and Maryland, has identified where Neotropical songbird migrants were most numerous on the Delmarva and Cape May peninsulas and what habitats they used. The project was an attempt to set priorities for acquisition and regulation.

Habitat destruction is a far more insidious threat to migrating birds than shooting or tower kills: people simply do not equate new homes and shopping malls with the shooting of birds. Construction

Cape May, the biggest funnel for migrating birds in the New World, is being paved and bulldozed for houses, roads, and shopping centers. Such developments (shown gray) destroy stopover habitat for birds, which have not evolved alternative routes or strategies to survive without it.

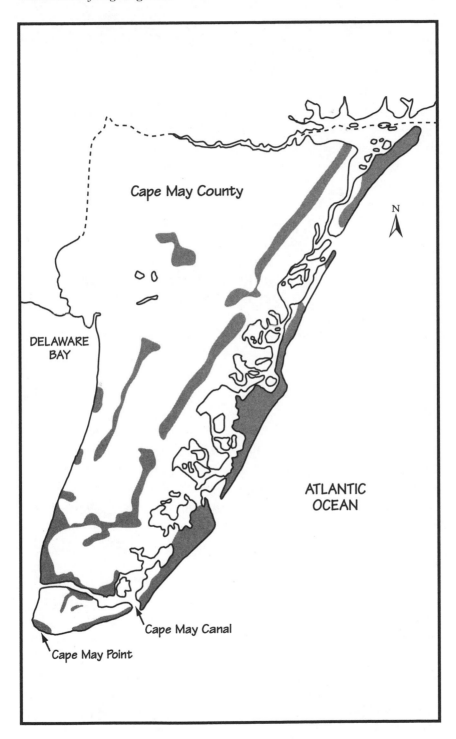

Cape May County

DELAWARE
BAY

ATLANTIC
OCEAN

N

Cape May Canal

Cape May Point

is legal and socially acceptable, but it has the same effect. I am baffled by people who condemn hunting but are mute when it comes to habitat destruction, filling wetlands, and managing habitat improperly. I can only presume that they do not equate unplanned development and habitat destruction with the killing of animals. Habitat destruction is clean—there is no blood. I once heard a developer say that there was plenty of habitat across the road from his site and that the birds could move. I guess he never played musical chairs.

HABITAT ENHANCEMENT

Acquisition of habitat is, without a doubt, the best means of protecting it for migrating birds. Acquisition is costly, however, and not all habitats are for sale. In addition to the outright purchase of habitat, management or enhancement of private land is effective in providing habitat for migrating birds. But unless it is deed restricted or protected by wetlands laws (which are not always enforced) or other regulations, most habitat that remains in private ownership is relatively unprotected. Management can be done at many levels. From the forester who manages thousands of acres to the homeowner who manages a 50-by-100-foot lot, habitat enhancement for migrating birds can make a difference.

With the realization that the habitats used by some migrating birds are threatened, habitat enhancement programs are being implemented by both private and public agencies. Often called backyard habitat programs because they target the owners of single-family homes, they are providing habitat for migrating hummingbirds and songbirds, as well as butterflies—species small enough to be able to forage in a hedgerow or tangle of brush that has been planted or let grow for this purpose.

Backyard habitat programs, such as those implemented by the National Wildlife Federation, the Cape May Bird Observatory, Chesapeake Bayscapes, some states, and others, are helping owners of homes, businesses, and public land landscape their properties in ways that meet the needs of migrants. Whether applicable throughout the United States and Canada, like the National Wildlife Federation's Backyard Habitat Program, or tailored for a specific region, like the Cape May Bird Observatory's Backyard Habitat Program, these programs all emphasize providing water, food, and—sometimes the most important—shelter. Shrubs, vines, and trees offer migrants protection from predators, wind, and rain, and a few fruiting or flowering trees or shrubs can make a small lot very attractive to migrants. A blank expanse of lawn, in contrast, is a sterile place.

THE CUMULATIVE EFFECTS OF HUMAN ACTIVITY

Does the loss of the migrants shot each year have a negative impact on migrant populations? Do tower kills take significant numbers of birds? Examined separately, neither of these causes of mortality is a serious threat: bird populations are fairly resilient and can recover from many losses. But the cumulative effect of shooting, tower kills, and window kills probably *is* significant, especially when combined with other killers of migrants, such as habitat destruction.

Similarly, the effect on migrant bird populations of cutting one forest of a few hundred acres in South America, North America, or along the migration pathways is negligible. But we have destroyed large forested tracts, countless small tracts, and enormous amounts of habitat along the migration pathways, and the effects are cumulative.

Because the destruction of a small tract will not be devastating to migrants, we often hear a developer argue that his project will cause no adverse environmental impact. The next developer says the same thing. Before long, hundreds and even thousands of tracts have been stripped of their vegetation. It is nearly impossible to get laws and regulations enacted that consider cumulative effects. It is also difficult to get a judge or regulatory agency to rule that a given project cannot be built based on its role in the scheme of cumulative habitat destruction. Our laws are such that we look at each project individually, without considering its effect in the overall scheme of development or land-use planning. Judges, prosecutors, and regulatory agencies are reluctant to act against single developers or small developments because they fail to realize the cumulative effect of these projects. Developers are now arguing that the regulation of their land by environmental agencies, usually with respect to wetlands laws, constitutes illegal taking under the Fourth Amendment of the U.S. Constitution. If their claim is upheld, does this mean that we cannot legislate or regulate land usage? Do zoning and other land-use laws and regulations constitute an illegal taking? Until the situation changes, we are going to lose many more migrants.

ECONOMICS AS A CONSERVATION TOOL

Birds are seldom considered an economic resource, except perhaps for poultry, those birds that are hunted, and birds that reduce insect pests. Nevertheless, birds generate billions of dollars through the purchase of paraphernalia and feed bought by birders and others who love these animals. One of the most important ways birds and birding generate economic revenue is through tourism by people who want to see birds. Birding is now a big business. Many birders easily spend $1,500 on a birding trip—lodging, meals, guide services, souvenirs, books, car rentals, and field guides, not to mention airfare.

Why do I mention birding tourism (now called avitourism) in a chapter on the conservation of migrating birds? The answer is simple. Birds need places in which to make stopovers, and birders need places to watch those birds. Migration stopover sites are frequented by birding tourists, and the money these birders generate is one argument for not destroying habitat at those sites. If the birds can draw avitourists to an area, they will provide needed economic revenue for the communities nearby. It is also a clean industry. Birding tourism does not require much in the way of buildings and supervisory staff, so these areas do not require the heavy infrastructure that some tourist destinations do. All that birders need is undisturbed, open space with parking, trails, viewing areas, and restrooms.

Avitourism is part of the larger phenomenon of ecotourism— travel to see wildlife and natural scenery. Many ecotourists today are birders. Migrating birds are an attraction that compels birders to travel hundreds or thousands of miles to sites around the world. Hawk Mountain Sanctuary, the Cape May peninsula, Point Pelee in Ontario, the Ramsey Canyon Preserve in Arizona, and the Lower Rio Grande Valley in Texas: all are visited by tens of thousands of birding tourists each year.

How many people visit these places? What is the seasonal visitation? How much do these people spend during their visits? In 1992 the U.S. Fish and Wildlife Service estimated that 100,000 birders visited the Cape May peninsula. Each year the number of birders who visit Cape May increases, however, so this statistic is already out of date. As of 1993, Hawk Mountain Sanctuary in Pennsylvania attracted 70,000 birders per year; the Nature Conservancy's Ramsey Canyon Preserve in Arizona, more than 30,000; J. N. "Ding" Darling National Wildlife Refuge in Florida, 750,000; Point Pelee National Park in Ontario, 60,000; and Forsythe National Wildlife Refuge (formerly called Brigantine NWR) in New Jersey, 175,000. And those are just the sites for which we have figures—for many other popular places, we have no idea how many birders visit each year.

The revenue that comes into these sites from birders varies, although it is safe to say that all generate millions of dollars each year for the surrounding communities. Each year at Cape May, birders spend about $10 million, mostly between September and May—the off-season for beach tourism. They come for autumn hawks, wintering seabirds, and spring warblers and shorebirds. By having this revenue, many motel and restaurant owners have made money on birders and as a result have become outspoken conservationists. At Point Pelee, where about 80 to 90 percent of the birding tourism occurs within two months, birders bring $2 million to $3 million in April and May, when the warblers migrate through. This augments a summer tourist economy that depends on a nearby national park.

At Hawk Mountain Sanctuary more than half the visitors come in September, October, and November, when hawks are migrating. Jim Brett, curator of Hawk Mountain Sanctuary, and I are struck by the numbers of people who come from far beyond the borders of Pennsylvania. It is likely that this privately owned sanctuary draws more than $2 million to the local economy each year.

The study of birding economics, as well as the attitudes of birders toward wildlife programs, can only lead to better conservation practices. Birding is a big business, one that can provide the impetus or funds for conservation. We should use the information to advocate more and better protection of existing open space, to help preserve migrating birds.

EDUCATING THE PUBLIC ABOUT MIGRANTS

Many of the dangers faced by migrating birds can be prevented or ameliorated. Before the steps can be taken to protect migratory birds, however, people must know more about the birds and their migrations. Just as people are being educated about the destruction of tropical rain forests, so too can they learn about the needs of migrating birds. Education programs of all sorts are necessary, although many are already operating and only need to be modified.

There are few full-scale educational programs that focus on migrating birds, but National Audubon, the National Fish and Wildlife Foundation's Partners in Flight program, and the New Jersey Audubon Society, among other groups, provide information packets on the subject. New Jersey Audubon is one of the few conservation organizations that offer publications dealing exclusively with the conservation of birds during migration; *New Jersey at the Crossroads of Migration* (1989) is a guide for general readers, including land-use planners, policy makers, wildlife managers, and birders.

EPILOGUE

The next time you are outdoors during a night or day of migration, consider what is happening. Look and listen for migrants. Watch them if you can. When you hear or see a migrant, think about what it is doing, how many millennia its kind have been migrating, and how it has evolved such a marvelous and difficult journey. As you ponder migration, think about all the various aspects of this phenomenon. I hope that by reading this book and by watching birds migrate, you will marvel, as I do, at the wonder of migratory birds.

RECOMMENDED RESOURCES

THIS BOOK DOES NOT PURPORT TO PRESENT EVERYTHING THAT IS known about migration, so I have prepared the following list of fifty books and articles that I think present the best overview of the field and will prove helpful to readers who wish to learn more. Some of the references are necessarily technical, but even these can be understood by readers who are patient and interested.

This list is biased by what I think is more important. Some references were included because they were written or edited by key players in migration research. Works published before 1980 or so may be outdated but give perspective to the field. Books that I highly recommend received that rating because they are well written and cover a topic without being overly technical. The *Scientific American* articles are especially readable.

Able, K.P. 1980. Mechanisms of orientation, navigation, and homing. In *Animal Migration, Orientation, and Navigation,* ed. S. A. Gauthreaux, Jr., 283–373. Academic Press, New York.

This lengthy chapter in a technical volume develops a theory regarding the hierarchy of orientation cues used by migrants.

Able, K. P., and V. P. Bingman. 1987. The development of orientation and navigation behavior in birds. *Quarterly Review of Biology* 62:1–29.

This important, technical review examines the development of orientation capabilities in birds. The authors conducted some of the seminal work in this field, showing the immense difficulties in studying ontogeny and migration.

Alerstam, T. 1990. *Bird Migration*. Cambridge University Press, New York.

English translation of a 1982 Swedish tome. The price is prohibitive, but this book may be the most complete volume on migration ever published. Alerstam, from Sweden, is the leading bird migration biologist in the world.

Baker, R. R. 1981. *The Mystery of Migration*. Viking Press, New York.

A coffee-table book.

Berthold, P. 1990. Spatiotemporal programs and genetics of orientation. *Experientia* 46:363–371.

A short article in a technical journal. Berthold, from Germany, is one of the world's foremost researchers in the field of migration physiology and the genetic basis of orientation and navigation.

—————. 1993. *Bird Migration*. Oxford University Press, New York.

This book promises to be an important, though technical, contribution.

Blem, C. 1980. The energetics of migration. In *Animal Migration, Orientation and Navigation,* ed. S. A. Gauthreaux, Jr., 175–224. Academic Press, New York.

A good but technical description of this topic.

Brett, J. 1991. *The Mountain and the Migration*. Cornell University Press, Ithaca, New York.

An informative and delightful history of the place where hawk watching was born and a fine introduction to hawk migration. Easy reading. Highly recommended.

Broun, M. 1949. *Hawks Aloft: The Story of Hawk Mountain*. Dodd, Mead, New York.

For years this wonderful book was the classic work on hawk migration, although biased to ridges. Easy reading.

Curry-Lindahl, K. 1981. *Bird Migration in Africa: Movements between Six Continents.* Vols. I and II. Academic Press, New York.

Perhaps the only book that deals with the biogeography, ecology, and evolution of an entire migration system. Highly recommended, especially for readers curious about migration in the Old World.

Dorst, J. 1962. *The Migration of Birds.* Houghton, Mifflin, Boston, Massachusetts.

A classic work on migration by one of the leading authorities on migration. Lots of information on Europe.

Dunne, P. J., R. Kane, and P. Kerlinger. 1990. *New Jersey at the Crossroads of Migration.* New Jersey Audubon Society, Franklin Lakes, New Jersey.

This short book summarizes bird migration in New Jersey with an emphasis on conservation of habitats needed by birds. Very readable, timely, and applicable anywhere birds migrate. Highly recommended.

Eastwood, E. 1967. *Radar Ornithology.* Methuen, London.

The only book about radar ornithology, this account traces the field from its inception, giving overviews of what was learned about migration from early radar studies.

Emlen, S. T. 1975. The stellar-orientation system of a migratory bird. *Scientific American* 233(2):102–111.

Excellent reading. Today, many biologists are not as convinced about the star compass, favoring magnetic cues. Don't rule out stars yet, however.

Experientia. Vol. 46, 1990.

A set of the most up-to-date technical scientific reviews of the orientation and navigation systems of birds. Great review papers by the key players in the field.

Gauthreaux, S. A., Jr. 1978a. The ecological significance of social dominance. In *Perspectives in Ethology,* ed. P. P. G. Bateson and P. H. Klopfer, 17–54. Plenum Press, New York.

Excellent technical review of a topic that is of growing concern to migration biologists.

———. 1978b. The influence of global climatological factors on the evolution of bird migratory pathways. In *Proceedings of the International Ornithological Congress* 17:517–525.

By examining prevailing winds, the author of this technical article makes conclusions regarding the evolution of migration pathways.

————. 1982. The ecology and evolution of avian migration systems. In *Avian Biology,* ed. J. R. King, D. S. Farner, and K. Parks, 6:93–168. Academic Press, New York.

This lengthy, technical review is one of the best.

Greenberg, R., and J. Reaser. 1995. *Bring Back the Birds: What You Can Do to Save Threatened Species.* Stackpole, Mechanicsburg, Pennsylvania.

Griffin, D. R. 1964. *Bird Migration.* Doubleday, Garden City, New York.

This short but classic work was at one time the finest book on bird migration.

Gwinner, E. 1990. *Bird Migration.* Springer Verlag, New York.

A compendium of scientific literature by many researchers in the field. The papers are technical but cover the most recent developments in bird migration.

Hagan, J. R., T. L. Lloyd-Evans, and J. Atwood. 1991. The relationship between latitude and the timing of spring migration of North American landbirds. *Ornis Scandinavica* 22:129–136.

Differences in seasonal duration of timing is compared for long- and short-distance migrant songbirds in spring. This short article in a technical journal includes thorough documentation through a long-term banding study at Manomet Bird Observatory.

Heintzelman, D. S. 1975. *Autumn Hawk Flights: The Migrations in Eastern North America.* Rutgers University Press, New Brunswick, New Jersey.

A classic account of hawk migration counting and what was known about hawk migration at the time. Although outdated, the book is fun reading.

Keast, A., and E. Morton. 1980. *Migrant Birds in the Neotropics.* Smithsonian Institution Press, Washington, D.C.

Dedicated mostly to the ecology of Neotropical migrants once they are in the tropics, this book provides insight as to the ecological problems migrants face en route. A few of the articles within this volume are devoted to migratory ecology and behavior.

Kerlinger, P. 1989. *Flight Strategies of Migrating Hawks.* University of Chicago Press, Chicago, Illinois.

This lengthy, technical volume parallels the structure of this book but focuses on the flight behavior of hawks.

Kerlinger, P., and M. R. Lein. 1986. Differences in winter range among age-sex classes of Snowy Owls *Nyctea scandiaca* in North America. *Onis Scandinavica* 17:1–7.

An example of a study that used migration specimens to examine the differential migration of a species by age and sex. A short article in a technical journal.

Kerlinger, P., and F. R. Moore. 1989. Atmospheric structure and avian migration. In *Current Ornithology,* ed. D. M. Power, 6:109–142. Plenum Press, New York.

This lengthy, technical review is very different from previous reviews of the topic. For the reader interested in the atmosphere as it affects migrating birds.

Ketterson, E. D., and V. Nolan, Jr. 1983. The evolution of differential bird migration. In *Current Ornithology,* ed. R. F. Johnston, 357–402. Plenum Press, New York.

This may be the best review of the hypotheses that seek to explain differential migration. Highly recommended.

Kramer, G. 1957. Recent experiments on bird orientation. *Ibis* 101:399-416.

Description in a technical journal of some of the early sun compass orientation experiments by one of the pioneers in the field. Highly recommended.

Lincoln, F. C. 1952. *Migration of Birds.* Doubleday, Garden City, New York.

As one of the first popular books on migration, this volume provided a wealth of information to those interested in migration before modern studies.

Matthews, G. V. T. 1955. *Bird Navigation.* Cambridge University Press, Cambridge, Massachusetts.

This early attempt to explain navigation behavior reviews much of the early literature and ideas.

McClure, H. E. 1974. *Migration and Survival of the Birds of Asia.* U.S. Army Medical Component, South East Asia Treaty Organization Medical Project, Bangkok, Thailand.

An abundance of distribution maps and banding recoveries are used by McClure to show the movements of some species of Asian birds. The maps are interesting because they show migration pathways that are not described elsewhere.

Mead, C. 1983. *Bird Migration.* Facts on File Publications, New York.

This is a fun book on migration but is poorly organized.

Moore, F. R. 1976. The dynamics of seasonal distribution of Great Lakes Herring Gulls. *Bird-Banding* 47:141–159.

The banding data analyzed by Moore is the best data set on differential migration by age classes of a species. A short article in a technical journal.

———. 1987. Sunset and the orientation behaviour of migrating birds. *Biological Reviews* 62:65–86.

A readable review of some fascinating aspects of orientation and migration.

Moore, F. R., and P. Kerlinger. 1987. Stopover and fat deposition by North American Wood-Warblers (Parulinae) following spring migration over the Gulf of Mexico. *Oecologia* 74:47–54.

An empirical study of stopover and fat deposition by warblers following trans-Gulf spring migration. A short article in a technical journal.

Moreau, R. D. 1953. *The Palearctic-African Bird Migration Systems.* Academic Press, New York.

This book is not difficult reading and addresses some interesting aspects of migratory biology.

Myers, J. P. 1984. Sex and gluttony on Delaware Bay. *Natural History* (May) 69–76.

Excellent popular article about an amazing phenomenon. If you read only one article about shorebird stopover ecology, this should be it.

Newton, I. 1979. *Population Ecology of Raptors.* Buteo Books, Vermillion, South Dakota.

Although this fine book is not about migration, it is one of the first to integrate aspects of breeding and nonbreeding ecology with migration behavior and ecology for a given taxon of birds. Highly recommended for people interested in raptors.

Pennycuick, C. J. 1969. The mechanics of migration. *Ibis* 111: 525–556.

An excellent introduction to the flight and energetics of migration. Technical but understandable.

———. 1972. *Animal Flight.* Edward Arnold, London.

This short book is perhaps the best on the subject. It is technical yet readable. Pennycuick is the world's authority on animal flight. Highly recommended.

Pennycuick, C. J., T. Alerstam, and B. Larsson. 1979. Soaring migration of the Common Crane *Grus grus* observed by radar and from an aircraft. *Ornis Scandinavica* 10:241–251.

A remarkable study of a soaring migrant. Flocks were followed for many miles—details on altitude, speed, flocking, and soaring behavior are given in this short article in a technical journal.

Poole, A. F., and B. Agler. 1987. Recoveries of ospreys banded in the United States, 1914–1984. *Journal of Wildlife Management* 51:148–156.

If you want to see how nicely banding data can be used to study migration pathways and distributions, read this paper. Poole's book on Ospreys is also excellent reading.

Porter, R., and I. Willis. 1968. The autumn migration of soaring birds at the Bosphorus. *Ibis* 110:520–536.

Easy-to-read documentation of migration through the Middle East, with lists of species, numbers, and dates.

Raveling, D. G. 1976. Migration reversal: A regular phenomenon of Canada geese. *Science* 193:153–154.

One of the first treatments of reverse migration.

Ridgely, R., and G. Tudor. 1990. *The Birds of South America.* University of Texas Press, Austin, Texas.

This is not a book on migration, but the species distribution maps are an excellent source of information on the migratory tendency and movements of some South American birds.

Safriel, U. 1968. Bird migration at Eilat, Israel. *Ibis* 110:283–320.

Numbers, species, and dates of migration through spring in Israel.

Stull, R. B. 1988. *An Introduction to Boundary-Layer Meteorology.* Kluwer Academic Publications, Dordrecht, Netherlands.

This may be the best book on the boundary layer. For students of bird migration, it is mandatory reading.

Terrill, S. B., and R. D. Ohmart. 1984. Facultative extension of fall migration by yellow-rumped warblers *(Dendroica coronata). Auk* 101:427–438.

Perhaps the best study of reinitiation (facultative initiation) of migration during midwinter by a songbird.

Tucker, V. A. 1970. The energetics of bird flight. *Scientific American* 220:70–79.

This article is a fine introduction to the energetics of bird flight. Readable and highly recommended.

Ulfstrand, S., G. Roos, T. Alerstam, and L. Osterdahl. 1974. Visible bird migration at Falsterbo *Fagelvarld,* supplement 8:1–245.

Although this publication is a supplement from a journal, it is really a book summarizing the seasonal timing of migrating birds during autumn at Falsterbo, Sweden—the European equivalent of Cape May, New Jersey.

Williams, T. C., and J. M. Williams. 1978. An oceanic mass migration of land birds. *Scientific American* 239:166–176.

The long jump of land birds between eastern North America and northern South America during autumn is summarized. Highly recommended.

INDEX